Propaganda, Public Diplomacy and Idea Invasion

THE STORY OF USIA'S WORLDNET

Donna Vincent Roa, PhD, ABC, CDPM®

PROPAGANDA, PUBLIC DIPLOMACY AND IDEA INVASION: THE STORY OF USIA'S WORLDNET

Bulk Sales and Speaker Bookings: Corporations and associations interested in discounts for bulk quantity purchases or an event speaker, please contact Donna Vincent Roa at 1-818-397-9867.

This book is based on the dissertation research conducted by the author for partial fulfillment of the requirements for the Degree of Doctor of Philosophy from the University of Southern Mississippi. Please consider leaving a review wherever you bought the book.

Cover Design: Sherman Soy | www.sherwinsoy.com
Editorial Review: Alex Roa

ISBN-10: 0-9907331-2-2
ISBN-13: 978-0-9907331-26

Dedication

To my husband Victor Roa, my bedrock and best friend who gives me the love and freedom to carry out my ideas no matter how outrageous. And to my children, Alexander Theodore Roa and Gretchen Marie Roa, who bring life to life for us and respect the creative process and the time investment it takes.

Abstract

PROPAGANDA, PUBLIC DIPLOMACY AND IDEA INVASION
THE STORY OF USIA'S WORLDNET

Established in 1953 as the nation's public relations agency, the United States Information Agency was sanctioned for nation branding, creating and modulating America's reputation, and spreading the good news about America to overseas audiences.

In the center of semantic debates and always operating under an expanding mosaic of labels and terminologies, USIA benefitted from public diplomacy's tremendous growth during President Reagan's historic mission of fighting communism. While many agencies experienced budgetary cuts, the USIA budget increased more than 80 percent, and some of those funds were used to finance Worldnet.

Created by USIA Director Charles Z. Wick and staff, Worldnet was the agency's attempt to use satellite television as an instrument of public diplomacy. Filled with compelling stories from insiders, this book lifts the veil on and provides a historically grounded introduction to Worldnet, the "jewel of the crown" of the Reagan administration's enchantment with aggressive political propaganda techniques.

In November 1983, Worldnet operations were established. Five years later, the service was severely restricted and nearly cancelled altogether. Though Worldnet was only one small component of USIA public diplomacy efforts, the questions surrounding the service's design, development, and existence and its institutional history are noteworthy.

This book examines the history and evolutions of propaganda and public diplomacy, provide an accounting of Worldnet's institutional history and complicated story, and documents USIA's efforts at using international television broadcasting for public diplomacy.

Acknowledgements

My sincere and heartfelt thanks go to my late wonderful parents, Margie Broussard Vincent and Ronald Gene Vincent, who taught me the value of hard work and learning, gave me the permission to ask why and explore life's possibilities, instilled in me the determination to succeed despite all odds, and encouraged me to look at life with joyful spirit, a million glasses half full, and a sense of humor.

To my sister Julie Matte, one of Louisiana's great educators and school administrators, who contributes an unwavering belief in my capacity to consistently achieve great things.

To Arlene Brown, my college forensics and debate coach, dear friend, and kindred spirit who has mentored and supported me throughout my academic career, my multipotentialite professional life and beyond. Her perspectives, thoughtful advice and gentle Southern manner have served as a consistent anchor for me over the past 40 years. I have been blessed to have such a friend in my life and cherish our continuing conversations beyond measure.

I would also like to acknowledge the contributions of the late Charles Wick, former USIA Director. I visited Charlie – one of the most dynamic, energetic, and articulate men that I have ever met – on the lot in his office at Fox Studios in California and interviewed him for this book. He was gracious and excited that I was focusing my research on Worldnet and was pleased to take part in the project.

Though years had passed since his tenure at USIA, he still showed a deep passion for its mission and purpose and the work he set out to accomplish and achieved. He also expressed many fond memories of those who served with him at the agency.

Finally, I would also thank Sherwood Demitz, who led USIA's Office of Media Research and later was my fantastic direct supervisor during my tenure at USIA, and the numerous USIA employees who allowed me to interview them about their leadership and involvement with Worldnet.

Finally, I am forever indebted to Bill Franco, former Special Assistant to Director Wick during the Reagan years. Bill introduced me to Worldnet.

Table of Contents

Why This Book

Each time I sit down to write a book, I often reflect on the reason I chose the topic. What made this topic compelling and one that I would devote countless hours to researching the story and defining and refining my ideas? What sparked this journey and inspired this effort?

In 1983, I was selected as a Rotary Scholar to study in England for the 1984-85 academic year. At the time of the award, I was a recent Louisiana State University graduate who had only travelled to Mexico for vacation, Kentucky for a 4-H exchange program, and Cocoa Beach, Florida to witness the Apollo-Soyuz space launch. I was also working for Conoco Refinery as an operator (hard hat and steel toe boots!) in the acid processing unit when I received the letter that I had been selected for an all-expense paid year abroad at the University of Hull in Hull, England.

As you might imagine, I was thrilled, excited and very happy to leave shift work behind.

Rotary Scholars have the luxury of being more than a student and more than a tourist in the home country. The Rotarians treat you like royalty and want your stay in their country to be the best possible. The scholarship requirement of giving speeches to Rotary Clubs in every city that you visit gave me the opportunity to interact with hundreds of Rotarians and experience hundreds of perspectives. I was intrigued and energized with what I learned.

This year abroad sparked my interest in international communication. CNN was in its infancy and not available on British television stations, so I started listening to Voice of America to stay connected to the home front. In 1985, VOA Europe broadcast to AM, FM and cable affiliates. Distinctly American with its contemporary format using live DJs, the service sought to gently invade the minds of the listener with American ideas, principles, culture, news, and policy discussions. I experienced international broadcasting from the other side and was fascinated with its potential to influence.

I travelled to Liverpool to take the GRE with the intention of applying for a doctoral program in international communication. I got accepted at three universities and chose the University of Southern Mississippi. It was close to home and the university offered me a very nice teaching stipend and package.

That fall, I started classes and study in the quiet town of Hattiesburg, MS and began my research. I focused on a wide variety of topics: the intersection of cultural and international affairs, the role communication plays in peacekeeping and diplomatic relations, how communication supports international trade, the value of brand identity in global business operations, public diplomacy, propaganda and international broadcasting.

My research also focused the evolution of labels used to describe how governments share ideas and information, how those words stirred heated intellectual debates, informed or destabilized compromise, and created embittered and divisive disputes between countries and governments. Through this early research and genuine intellectual connection to the great communication philosophers and theoreticians, I landed on the examination of USIA's Worldnet.

What makes this book different is that I had the chance to personally speak with many of the players involved in the story of Worldnet. I complemented extensive desk and archival research with in-person interviews.

I sat with Charlie Wick, former director of USIA appointed by the President, when he was an executive at Fox Studios in Los Angeles and spent many hours with him discussing his role at USIA, his relationship with President Reagan, and how he viewed the importance of global broadcasting and communication. Much had been written about Charlie in the press, some articles not so positive, and I felt like I needed to give him the chance to articulate his side of the story.

I drove to Washington, DC from Hattiesburg, MS during the Christmas semester break for the in-person interviews and stayed at the lovely Thompson Markward Hall, a Young Women's Christian Home chartered by Congress in 1887 near Union Station in Washington, DC. I was able to conduct the bulk of the interviews the first week I was in town. Charlie's interview was on the first part of the third week. On Thursday of the first week, I received a call from his assistant that Charlie had had to fly back to

California and requested that I meet him in Los Angeles for the interview.

I paused on the phone and took a deep breath and thought about the logistics quandary. I was a poor graduate student with no extra funds for plane fare who had just driven to DC from Hattiesburg and now my opportunity to interview THE person who led the Worldnet story required that I drive from Washington, DC to Los Angeles to make it happen.

I had to say yes. I would do everything within my power to get to Los Angeles. I had to interview Charlie Wick. My story wouldn't complete if I didn't have his voice represented in it.

While I would never, ever do it again, I did drive from Washington, DC to Los Angeles for the interview with Charlie (he insisted that I call him that). The investment in time and effort was sincerely worth it. Charlie was a force. I met the man I had read so much about and was able to see how his energy, forcefulness and aggressiveness positioned him to make things happen on Capitol Hill, while at the same time piss a few people off and get him into trouble. I could certainly understand that dynamic.

I am honored to have had the chance to speak with him and to explore the full battery of questions that I had devised from my research effort. He hesitated on none of them and welcomed my reaching back out to him if I needed more information. Traipsing across the United States to speak with Charlie was indeed worth the effort.

⌘

While Worldnet was only one small component of an enormous public diplomacy apparatus, it was an important part of the U.S. Government's public diplomacy efforts designed to support American policies abroad. The story surrounding its design, development, and existence deserves to be told.

The critical goal of this book is to provide an accounting of Worldnet's institutional history and to yield more than just the partial story told in the popular press. The research for this book covers the time span of November 1983 to October 1988 and includes desk and archival research, observation and personal interviews.

Many articles about Worldnet have been written in the popular press, yet no detailed accounting of its history exists, and little has been written about the institution's inception, operation and near demise. I examined Worldnet through the lens of two important terms – propaganda and public diplomacy. I explored and analyzed policy-related semantics and labeling, the administrative framework of the labeling, and how it affected policies, opinions and attitudes related to international communication.

I have included a evidence of government information activities and the precursor organizations of USIA (i.e., The Creel Committee, Office of Facts and Figures, and the Office of War Information); an analysis of propaganda and public diplomacy; and an exploration of the policy factors and world events that altered the structure of U.S. information institutions, including USIA and Worldnet.

The book also offers a brief history of external governmental communication efforts operating under the label of propaganda and includes a cursory explanation of the dynamics of the interactions between various governmental bodies, highlights methods of propaganda used during wartime, and addresses major organizational developments, including the establishment of the

United States Information Agency. Program limitations, effects, and influence are also covered.

The book examines public diplomacy in light of U.S. national security efforts within the context of USIA — the agency that focuses on the government-to-people aspects of diplomacy. It showcases the piecemeal strategy of the United States information activities, how USIA adjusted to national circumstances and pressures, in addition to providing a critique on the political dynamics of communication institutions and how those institutions became a manifestation of the political environment and political process.

For this project, I read thousands of pages of articles in the popular press, news briefs issued by the USIA, books, backgrounders and Congressional testimony. The complementary in-person interviews with key players in the Worldnet story unearthed additional, important insights. It is this for this reason that I have written *Propaganda, Public Diplomacy and Idea Invasion: The Story of USIA's Worldnet.* I hope you enjoy the evidence of the journey.

>   — *Donna Vincent Roa, PhD, ABC, CDPM®*

INTRODUCTION

Telling America's Story

During times of war, governments and countries use propaganda to field controversy and increase international tensions. Though the printed media in the early 1920s had the ability to reach large audiences, it was not until the late 1930s with the introduction of radio, film, and the expansion and systematization of advertising that the mass audience became a reality. Totalitarian dictatorships and democratic regimes began to use these new channels to propagandize the mass audience.

In the 1940s, the "cold war" between societies began and information became a weapon for antagonism and counter-offensives. Propaganda was injected into the international environment at levels not experienced before, even during the two world wars.

The "war of wars" was the war of words – an idea invasion of sorts – between the United States and the Soviet Union that used distortion and force to convince others that the American government and its people were nothing more than a "power-hungry nation of warmongers." America concentrated on telling its story to the world to bolster U.S. foreign policy objectives.

In the fifties, radio broadcasting was used continually and regularly by all of the major nations of the world. With the outbreak of the Korean War, anti-American propaganda and other atrocity stories from the Soviet Union increased. American policy makers tried to rally and coordinate its propaganda efforts, but failed to produce any strategic or comprehensive efforts to match the output of the Soviets.

Radio Free Europe, which was sponsored by the National Committee for a Free Europe, went on the air in December 1949. Its psychological warfare was directed towards the Soviet Union and its European satellites. By 1956, its total production of programs exceeded 3,000 hours per week (Rubin, 1960).

From 1950 to 1960, accounts of organizational changes, of unsuccessful attempts to separate psychological strategy from national strategy, and of failed attempts to produce a comprehensive information program fill the history of the U.S. information program. Efforts to respond to the "red" threat were there, but more often than not, those efforts were unorganized.

The United States Information Agency (USIA) was created in 1953 to handle the U.S. government's overseas information program, and there was a gradual evolution towards a strategic approach to information. This government-run public relations agency for overseas audiences was expected to engage in soft-core or soft sell propaganda and American public diplomacy.

One year after the newly independent body was created, major problems confronted the organization: its budget was too small given the scope of its objectives, the content and character of its output, and the organization's overall effectiveness was questioned ("A Study," 1954). Additionally, from 1953 to 1960, the agency faced numerous problems ranging from unpopular directors and fluctuating appropriations to intense scrutiny from various congressional committees.

Notwithstanding, the new approach seemed to support U.S. national security objectives. Along with the Voice of America and other media supporting the U.S. efforts overseas, the USIS Public Affairs Officers (PAO) were enlisted in the battle for men's minds.

In the 1960s, USIA got high priority from the Kennedy Administration, and overall, the role of the agency was upgraded. Agency Director Edward R. Murrow was given full support from the President for the agency's attempts to respond to the threat of Communism. Director Leonard Marks focused efforts more on mutual understanding and the sharing of information and less effort towards persuasion and propaganda.

During the 1970s and 1980s, international radio broadcasting increased and the cold war of words continued. USIA operated as a "full-service" international communication institution, though still responsive and reactive in nature to the world and domestic political realities.

Domestic political realities continued to affect long-range planning and to interfere with information and propaganda activities. The agency also was affected by the ever-changing congressionally mandated rules and funding practices.

Since the agency's inception, Congressional appropriations committees evidently showed diminished understanding of the necessity for USIA, made decisions on the basis of political pressures, and created an atmosphere of insecurity within the agency with its various investigations. Adverse publicity and Congressional pressures also kept the program off-balance as the agency tried to adjust its policies and operations. Information funding, in general, was the victim of swings in official favor and disfavor.

Over the years, much significance was attached to the semantics surrounding the information program instead of on the implications and the consequences of a program that had the potential power of favorably influencing other nations and supporting U.S. national security efforts. Endless debates on the differences between education and information, propaganda and information, information and culture, policy information and general information, and propaganda and public diplomacy, ultimately did nothing to support or strengthen foreign policy objectives.

Satellite TV Supporting American Foreign Policy

Created by United States Information Agency Director Charles Z. Wick and staff, Worldnet was the agency's attempt to use satellite television as an instrument of public diplomacy that supported American foreign policy. Established in November 1983, Worldnet was put in operation to affect opinions, attitudes, and perceptions of peoples around the globe and serve as a major channel for USIA to "tell America's story abroad" and deliver the U.S. message overseas.

During its tenure, Worldnet grew to be the third largest satellite-delivered television network servicing Europe and was the world's first global government-owned satellite service.

Worldnet has been described as "the most phenomenal and ambitious undertaking in the history of television" and some officials called it the "jewel of the crown" of the Reagan administration's enchantment with aggressive propaganda techniques. USIA called Worldnet a tool of public diplomacy.

Worldnet was the sister broadcasting service to the Voice of America. In the phase of superpower ideological confrontation called the "Star Wars of Ideas," the international satellite television network became what some called a "defensive and offensive weapon in the war of ideas waged by the superpowers." It was another communication channel for USIA to expand its public relations efforts in support of modern diplomacy and deliver a broad, a pluralistic view of American life and values.

Worldnet, USIA's newest tool of public diplomacy, was also enmeshed in a variety of complex issues involving domestic politics and attitudes towards the information program in general. A victim of mostly official disfavor, many saw Worldnet as a misplaced effort in the agency's foreign information program. No records indicate that the service, in any way, intensified the debate regarding cultural sovereignty, cultural imperialism and domination, and the free flow of information.

U.S. Ambassador Geoffrey Swaebe noted that in Belgium, there were some initial reservations and skepticism about the service. Some thought that Worldnet's goal was to propagandize rather than to further understanding. The willingness of the U.S. government officials to be interviewed on the program coupled with the fact that the service offered in-depth question-and-answer sessions allayed those fears about its mission (Swaebe, 1986).

Wick explained that once governments knew and understood the interactive nature of the programs, realized that their news landscape could benefit from the products the service had to offer, and knew they would have control over what ultimately aired, they usually accepted the service's offerings.

Worldnet's teleconferencing capabilities supplied journalists with the chance to ask direct, uncensored questions to U.S. policy makers and other guests. While the viewer did shape the types and kinds of information imparted in the program, it was not a true, reciprocal dialogue. The interactives were merely a question and answer forum – similar to a staged news or information conference. All in all, there was not a true "equal opportunity" to share ideas.

To overcome some of these obstacles such as international treaty arrangements, USIA approached ministerial level officials directly, and asked for their permission to send the free, cross-border signals. Through these direct negotiations and a keen awareness of the various countries' regulatory environments, USIA sidestepped much of the traditional governmental reluctance to foreign broadcasts.

Critics argued that USIA, during the past 15 or so years, had focused on Soviet-oriented propaganda. The agency significantly expanded during the Reagan administration and found its strength in Reagan's historic mission of fighting communism. The anti-Communist stance of the administration coupled with the bold assertion of American hegemony brought both vitality and additional funding for stepped up international communication. The position was enhanced by U.S.' expanding interest in being the dominant player in the world information order, and the nation's emergence from detente and the post-Vietnamese war syndrome.

Not surprisingly, during the Reagan years, while many departments and agencies experienced budgetary cuts, USIA budget increased more than 80 percent, and some of those funds were used to finance Worldnet – the agency's newest international broadcasting channel.

Fifth Anniversary Marks Service Suspension

Ironically, on the fifth anniversary of Worldnet, the service was operating at far less than its full capacity. By October 1, 1988, Worldnet's passive programming (news and feature material) was suspended by the United States Congress with Public Law 100-204, a congressional mandate which some say jeopardized America's ability to reach foreign publics.

Alvin Snyder, former director of USIA's Television and Film Service, noted that the action was hasty, and was a setback for the United States information program. In November 1983, the Worldnet operations were established. Five years later, the service was severely restricted and nearly cancelled altogether.

On the surface, it seemed that United States' policy makers did not recognize and understand the importance of using television to support public diplomacy and propaganda efforts. But there was more to the story of what some described as the "government's number one communication weapon."

CHAPTER TWO

Political Atmosphere & Value-Laden Terminology

The field of international communication is highly fragmented and swimming in labels driven by the ideologies of practitioners and others who believe that everything we do needs a label or that giving something a new label changes the way we view it. Throughout history, you can see that one person's communication is another person's propaganda. One person's public relations is another person's public diplomacy. One person's war information is another person's international broadcasting, and it goes on.

Despite the evolution of the use and definitions of the myriad of labels, each stands for the propagation or dissemination of ideas and information. Communication, propaganda, public diplomacy, nation branding, war of words, idea invasion, public affairs, psychological warfare, public relations and others all use the same tools and method and each can be used to inform, influence and manipulate public opinion.

Communication, Propaganda and Public Diplomacy

From a review of the history of these words (i.e., communication, propaganda and public diplomacy for this analysis) in the Oxford English Dictionary, communication was used first in the late 13th century, propaganda about 300 years later, and public diplomacy around 1856 in its first use describing diplomacy conducted openly. In early December 1929, a Saturday Evening Post story connected public relations experts to propaganda and public diplomacy.

If you further examine the etymological history of propaganda, in its early use, it was first viewed only in the most neutral sense. Propaganda was part of social, religious and political systems throughout history and contemporary times. Then through the early 1900s, the label was weighed down with negative sentiment and was seen as nothing more than organized persuasion or suspicious rhetoric. This is a pure example of the evolution of a clearly neutral term into one that was imbued with tremendous negative baggage.

Even Joseph Goebbels disliked the word propaganda. In the early stages of his relationship with Hitler, he expressed his dislike for the word and firmly pushed back when Hitler suggested that the propaganda would be in the name of the agency that he

(Goebbels) would lead. Hitler believed that communication efforts during a war needed a powerful label and that propaganda could make a war more effective.

Interestingly, in later years, the word propaganda became closely associated with Goebbels and his intense and destructive communication efforts. The intent behind and the effects of his efforts further cemented the connection between propaganda and evil and helped to give propaganda a really bad name.

Though public diplomacy was used in a newspaper article in the mid-1800s, the phrase public diplomacy was not in the dictionary when this research project was started. One could find references to public diplomacy in books on international communication and each author proposed a definition unique to his or her perspective.

Value-laden terminologies used to a piercing volume and sophistication ultimately fractures the field. Definitions for these labels are changed or updated by authors, practitioners and communication critics who seek to add their special take on the label (or word), to attribute new meaning to the label or embed a new tone or sentiment, albeit negative, to the definition.

Image Shaping and A Dying Label

From 1914 to 1992, U.S. communication program goals and labels changed, ideological warfare efforts decreased, and options for communication with other countries increased. Not surprisingly, moving forward, propaganda was very seldom used as a label to describe U.S. overseas communication, information, and cultural activities. American strategists operated public diplomacy programs.

As Cold War tensions lessened and detente became a political reality, the word propaganda with its negative connotations and historical association with ideological crusades was no longer useful or necessary. Furthermore, the word propaganda did not adequately describe the new and varied activities of classical diplomacy and image shaping (i.e., those activities established to support enhanced communication and understanding). Most government officials and policy makers believed the use of the word propaganda was no longer appropriate.

The subject of propaganda was avoided until someone disagreed with those who operated in the public diplomacy realm or couldn't see the purpose or value of efforts labeled as public diplomacy. Some called public diplomacy "old wine in a new bottle," while others described it as psychological warfare that took advantage of the explosion of technology. Others continued called it outright propaganda.

The line between public diplomacy and propaganda was ever so fine. The political atmosphere abroad, the prevailing philosophy at USIA and within the White House, and the flavor of the day on Capitol Hill dictated whether or not USIA's efforts were labeled propaganda or public diplomacy. Always aware of that dynamic, USIA was usually low-key in its efforts to spread the good news about America.

Most would suggest that public diplomacy involved a variety of activities that would include international communication and cultural and educational activities in which the public was involved. Many authors connected the definition to influencing public attitudes on the formation and execution of foreign policies and cited public diplomacy as something that went beyond traditional diplomacy because it involved the public.

Unlike propaganda, which could be seen as a one-way stream of negative communication based on a distasteful intent, public diplomacy was a complement to traditional diplomacy because it moved beyond the one-to-one communication efforts and used technology and in-person exchanges to support the process. Across the map, public diplomacy's definitions and meaning expanded and contracted depending on the circumstance. Ultimately, its meaning remained somewhat elusive.

Public diplomacy, which implies no value judgment, was a safe and palatable euphemistic replacement for propaganda. But more importantly, the word had a neutral sentiment. Having the word diplomacy in the phrase seemingly protected it from adopting a negative sentiment.

Furthermore, having the word public as an adjective added the people element and made it personal. The phrase intimated involvement with the public and a potential opportunity for a two-way exchange of information.

Moreover, public diplomacy lacked distasteful history, and evolved as an acceptable term for describing information related activities for the latter part of the century. However, in the early years, recognition of its importance had not spread beyond those few government officials and academia kept tabs on its growth.

In the early eighties, most of the issuances and articles on public diplomacy came from the U.S. government, including The Advisory Commission on Public Diplomacy; the U.S. General Accounting Office; and the House of Representatives Subcommittee on International Operations. They used the public diplomacy label to describe the activities that the U.S. government and other organizations carried out overseas. The public diplomacy label also embraced the crucial and important political reality that public support had become an integral part of U.S. relations with other countries.

Finding a label substitute for propaganda that made everyone happy was not an easy task. Public diplomacy seemed like the classic, acceptable label for this new approach to foreign relations. It rightly incorporated government-to-people, people-to-government, and people-to-people educational and international communication activities used to influence public attitudes and educate foreign publics about U.S. policies.

Like propaganda, public diplomacy evolved into an important element of the U.S. foreign policy mechanism. As an all-inclusive term, public diplomacy developed a higher profile than propaganda, successfully incorporated elements of a diplomatic and foreign relations environment in flux, and allowed for a divergence of perceptions both within the Congress and within USIA.

Expanded communication technologies and the increasing importance of public opinion further compartmentalized diplomacy and gave public diplomacy a home. Indeed, the practices of traditional diplomacy were increasingly influenced by the interplay between the mass media and public opinion, just as the interplay had influenced the practices of traditional politics.

Contemporary diplomacy, with the aid of mass communication, had successfully morphed into the all-encompassing practice of public diplomacy.

Public diplomacy, which has been classified as a unique phenomenon, has roots in persuasion, the application of relationship building and the intention to share foreign policies and objectives within an international relations context. The overarching goal of public diplomacy is to change or affect public opinion, improve relationship dynamics, and stimulate positive exchanges.

While one can establish and support the argument that public diplomacy is a unique phenomenon, it is fundamentally both communication and public relations. Public diplomacy has the potential to impact the achievement of foreign policy goals and extend the reach of traditional diplomacy.

Policy makers believed that a systematic and sustained public diplomacy program could lessen the possibility of military conflict, and USIA was tagged when public diplomacy was elevated to address national securing concerns.

Where does Worldnet fit into this paradigm? Often called a tool of public diplomacy or nation branding, Worldnet was viewed as propaganda run by USIA's "psychological warfare experts." Castro described Worldnet a "means of ideological and cultural penetration (used) to sell the decadent Yankee way of life in our (sic) impoverished nations." One Soviet information official who called Worldnet television aggression from space maintained that "not since the time of the, Cold War, has there been such a massive, direct participation by U.S. leadership and top military men in the country's official propaganda." A West German journalist noted a widespread sense of astonishment that the United States would "imitate Moscow's ham-handed techniques in trying to shape the truth for its allies."

Everything is Communication

Harold Lasswell's definition of communication which states, "Who says what in which channel to whom and with what effects" is so broad that, in my opinion, it could encompasses communication, propaganda, public diplomacy, and all of the other labels that are associated with this kind of work. The cover of this book (background word fabric) itemizes the panoply of labels that have been given to communication at various points in history.

Study each term and you'll find that there is also significant overlap in the definitions, and across these labels, the variables still include: who, what they say, which channel they use, what audience they focus on, and what effect that message will have on the defined audiences.

What is missing in Lasswell's definition is the intention of the communicator. We shouldn't confuse intent with effect. The effect, which is difficult to measure, may or may not be connected to the intent of the communicator. If the effect were connected to the intent, then the communicator would deem the effort as successful.

Edward Bernay's definition of public relations includes the intent piece..."to engineer public support for an activity, cause, movement or institution." While it intimates intent, the definition does not include the nature or the spirit of the intention.

According to Aristotle, instruments of rhetoric can be manipulated to achieve either honest or dishonest ends. Aristotle also noted that accompanying circumstances were an important consideration in communication.

And that's how all of this becomes cloudy. If someone believes that the intention of the communicator is not honest or altruistic, it is very easy for him or her to default to any label that has negative connotations. For example, if you call something spin or propaganda, your intent in this labeling is to associate that action with either being wrong or something you don't agree with. Time and again throughout history, the back-and-forth with labels gave communication a bad name.

CHAPTER THREE

Propaganda & Technology

When information crossed borders, belligerents could exercise censorship. Information was gotten slowly and more often than not, with extreme difficulty. At the advent of international radio used during World Wars, the information flow situation changed radically.

The outbreak of World War I (1914-1918) created new facets of international broadcasting and increased the importance of public opinion. This cataclysmic event, which thrust information about the United States and other countries into the forefront of the minds of people throughout the world, marked the starting point for this chapter on propaganda.

Methods of propaganda used during this time profoundly influenced subsequent governmental communication efforts. Developments in mass communication provided a basis for the rapid growth in propaganda. International broadcasting became an important foreign policy mechanism of war.

Although limited to transmissions in Morse code and transmissions used intermittently in international disputes in World War I, propagandists used radio during World War II to deliver their political propaganda to the masses. Even though other methods were used, radio was, by far, the most important tool for propaganda. It became the "fifth arm of a nation's defense efforts" and an essential feature of modern political and international affairs.

As a direct consequence, there was an increased interest and involvement in political and foreign affairs. Additionally, countries could no longer control the information penetrating their borders or isolate their publics from information sent by other governments.

U.S. Efforts During World War I

On April 14, 1917, just eight days after World War I was declared, President Woodrow Wilson set up, by executive order, the first official U.S. propaganda office – the Committee on Public Information – to disseminate and propagandize the official point of view overseas, and to send selective information to the U.S. press. Members of the Committee were the Secretary of War, Secretary of the Navy, and George Creel, the Committee Chairman. The body was created to exploit Wilson's Fourteen Points in Europe – "to rally moral and domestic support on the home front" and to make "the geographically remote struggle in

Europe of immediate ideological relevance to the majority of the American people."

Some writers believed that the Fourteen Points were motivated by propaganda purposes. Others suggested that Wilson's Fourteen Points document was probably the most effective piece of international communication in the twentieth century.

The origin of the Fourteen Points is attributed to the American Commissioner of the Committee on Public Information in Petrograd who communicated the need for the president to give a message "in a thousand words or less, in short, almost placard-like paragraphs and short sentences" for purposes of rapid translation and dissemination.

George Creel, a man with strong political ties to President Wilson, was chosen to head the Committee on Public Information (a.k.a., the Creel Committee). Devoted to Wilsonian political doctrines, Creel had advocated Wilson's nomination for president, had assisted Wilson during his two presidential campaigns, and had contributed numerous press articles supporting Wilson's political ideas.

According to Josephus Daniels, Secretary of the Navy and a Wilson supporter, no other name was suggested as the executive head of that committee except George Creel who met the requirements posed by the Cabinet members.

To ensure that everyone in the United States, including foreign journalists, and everyone abroad understood why America was going to war, Creel was directed to mobilize and exploit the communication industry, and to use all forms of communication to spread the U.S. message (e.g., the printed word, spoken word, films, letters, wireless news services, balloons, and planes).

He also used the Division of Women's War Work to answer letters from soldier's loved ones, and involved painters, sculptors, designers, and cartoonists to further the cause of America.

The extensive propaganda efforts of George Creel's Committee on Public Information (CPI) stirred excessive emotions and hatred towards other nations, created a fear in America that propaganda should not serve as a formal instrument of foreign policy, and created a distrust of publicity techniques in general. The Committee's propaganda, which lacked credibility, elevated hopes and fostered a belief that America was fighting the war to end all wars.

The activities of this Committee gave the American people a taste of war propaganda – what one author described as "disturbing, though somewhat inaccurate, introduction to the force of propaganda in the modern world."

Additionally, Creel's activities choked the channels of communication with official news and opinions and were seen as a backhanded attempt at censorship of the domestic press. Not surprisingly, Creel was one of the most disliked members of the national government during the war and was described as too eager, too impetuous and as flamboyant.

Creel's CPI was an apt illustration of war propaganda and followed all of the precepts of Harold Lasswell's model for war propaganda: mobilizing hatred against the enemy, preserving the friendships of allies, procuring the cooperation of neutrals, and demoralizing the enemy. CPI's mission was to encourage, then consolidate and create a revolution of opinion that moved from seeing the U.S. as anti-militaristic to a highly organized war machine.

By 1919, the war was over, and Creel's organization was officially abolished. But, its efforts were not forgotten. The CPI was described as the "model for practically every plan of government public relations in the event of war." The CPI had a broad scope of activities not seen in another government agency and through its work established the model for government propaganda and public relations during war time.

U.S. War Propaganda Program

When the United States entered the war in 1941, government officials gave immediate consideration to the war propaganda program. In response to world activities and to the spread of fascist propaganda in Latin America, the United States set up the Interdepartmental Committee for Scientific Cooperation and a Division of Cultural Cooperation in the Department of State to focus on information and cultural activities in that region.

Formally called the Coordinator of Inter-American Affairs (CIAA) and headed by Nelson Rockefeller, the CIAA's objectives were to promote goodwill and dialogue between the nations of the western hemisphere and to counter Axis propaganda. The CIAA leased several of the dozen low-powered, commercially owned and operated transmitters throughout the United States to broadcast to the region and used the stations as a means to counter hostile propaganda from the Nazis.

Spurred by the Nazi threat to United States' security, Roosevelt also established The Coordinator of Information Office in July 1941 to carry out propaganda activities overseas. Its mission was to coordinate intelligence collection and analysis and to transmit information to areas outside of Latin America. Colonel William J.

Donovan, the individual who later headed the Office of Strategic Services, directed the office.

An integral part of the Coordinator of Information Office, Roosevelt's Foreign Information Service (FIS) had the mission of explaining U.S. objectives, spreading the gospel of democracy, and upholding the cause of the United States. Headed by Robert Sherwood and forbidden to engage in domestic information purveying, the FIS operated on the basic assumption that truth was the basis on which to build an American information program and that a democratic society should not undertake one that featured a Goebbels-type of deceptive propaganda. Sherwood established headquarters in New York City and after recruiting a staff, began producing radio materials (primarily news programs) to be broadcast on the privately owned shortwave stations.

When Germany declared war on the U.S. and Japan attacked Pearl Harbor, Sherwood moved quickly by hiring John Houseman to direct FIS radio operations.

In December, an FIS studio in San Francisco broadcast to Asia and two months later – 79 days after the U.S. entered the war – on February 24, 1942, the FIS broadcast to Europe via BBC medium and long wave transmitters.

In late 1941, Roosevelt established the Office of Facts and Figures, a precursor organization to other public information agencies. Directed by Archibald MacLeish, the office, which was originally destined to be a part of the office of Civilian Defense, was concerned primarily with enlisting domestic support for the defense program.

Roosevelt also established an Agency for Foreign Intelligence and Propaganda to focus on overseas propaganda activities. This would be the first and last time the word propaganda was used in the name of a government agency.

Office of War Information

By 1942, the President established the Office of War Information (OWI) with Order 9312 and gave the OWI full responsibility of managing both domestic and foreign propaganda activities. At the time, information and cultural programs were kept separate – information for the enemy and occupied territories, and cultural or education programs for the neutral states.

Elmer Davis, veteran journalist of newspaper and later television, was chosen to head the organization. Milton Eisenhower, younger brother of General Dwight Eisenhower, was chosen as Associate Director. Absorbing the Office of Facts and Figures, and the "Voice of America," which at this time was the title used to describe the collective output of the various shortwave commercial stations operating from the United States; the OWI was essentially an amalgamation of the U.S. government's public information activities.

The organization was responsible for conducting psychological warfare efforts abroad and for providing Americans with news about the war effort. The OWI's goal was to use propaganda as an offensive weapon and as an instrument of foreign policy.

Initially, the Office of War Information had few options for shortwave radio broadcasting. Only a dozen transmitters were available amounting to 50,000 watts of shortwave transmitting equipment, which was the same power as one large commercial station.

Robert Sherwood, who was head of the Overseas Branch (FIS), called on ABC, CBS, and a several other stations to offer their services and contribute to the war information effort in an effort to establish a formal broadcasting arm of the Office of War Information.

By November 1942, the Office of War Information took over the participating commercial shortwave facilities to unify the "Voice of America." As prescribed by the President, its mission was war propaganda.

Twenty-three transmitters were constructed, and by the time the Allied summit took place in Casablanca, the service was broadcasting in 27 languages. By 1943, the Voice of America service was utilizing 42 transmitters and broadcasting in 46 languages.

While the Office of War Information used radio as an aboveground information medium, the Office of Strategic Services (OSS) used radio exclusively for subversion. A separate branch of the OSS – the Morale Operations – was created to disseminate "secret propaganda...to incite and spread dissension, confusion, and disorder within enemy countries."

Created in June 1942 by President Roosevelt, the organization gathered and analyzed strategic information and guided U.S. "propaganda and warfare phases of psychological warfare even though the Joint Chiefs were uncertain as to what psychological warfare entailed."

By December 1942, the Joint Chiefs encouraged all forms of moral subversion with the issuance of Directive 144/11/D, and by the end of the war, the OWI had 13,000 employees in its domestic and overseas offices where the posts operated under the newly-minted name of United States Information Service (USIS). The largest part of all USIA activities is the USIS. Operating as an integral part of the U.S. diplomatic mission, USIS antedates USIA.

The OWI continued to operate with outdated wartime goals and responsibilities, but not for long.

By August 1945, the Office of War Information was liquidated and later that year, activities were sharply reduced by a Congress that was motivated by a strong dislike of propaganda.

The Voice of America (VOA) remained in operation broadcasting in 40 languages 24-hours-per-day, but many of the broadcast services were reduced or eliminated. In 1945, funds were reluctantly appropriated for VOA worldwide broadcasts and CIAA's broadcasts to Latin America. By the end of that year, the two organizations were transferred to the Department of State.

Peacetime Efforts

The years 1945 to 1948 marked a virtual disarmament of the U.S. "psychological" activities overseas and a marked hesitancy to support international broadcasting. Propaganda was no longer a valid instrument in times of peace. The President stymied most propaganda activities, and the U.S. program was reduced to educational exchanges and cultural exchanges and Radio in the American Sector (RIAS) in West Berlin. The service was set up in 1945 and continued to play an important role in maintaining the morale of the Berliners during the Berlin blockade.

A joint German and American venture, the peacetime operation had been initially designed to put pressure on the Soviet occupiers, to challenge the Communist monopoly of information on East Germany, to closely monitor the political situation in the Soviet Zone, and to keep the Communist leaders on the defensive.

Directed by Americans with the news prepared by a German staff, RIAS, which had a separate identity from the VOA, broadcast information through public address systems mounted on trucks. A model of low-key, informational programming, the station also broadcast news, a wide variety of music and features, and special programming such as "University of the Air."

Replacing the Office of War Information and overseeing the United States' information and cultural functions overseas, the Office of Information and Cultural Affairs was set up in the State Department in 1946. William Benton, the Undersecretary for Public and Cultural Affairs, overhauled the Office of Information and Cultural Affairs by removing all wartime functions and focusing goals on peacetime functions.

The new peacetime operation's foreign activities concentrated its diplomatic efforts beyond government-only contacts and interactions. The conduct of foreign affairs was changing.

Congressional Legislation

The first major legislative step in people-to-people diplomacy was the Fulbright Act of 1946. The legislation was set up for the sale of war surpluses to foreign governments. The funds generated from the sale were earmarked supporting an educational exchange program. In 1961, Congress created the related Fulbright-Hays Act to coordinate and simplify the administration of the exchange programs.

The second major piece of legislation affecting U.S. public diplomacy programs was the Smith-Mundt Act, which still serves as the basic legislation of the U.S. information program today.

The Smith-Mundt Act

Some credit the resurrection of the U.S. propaganda program to two Congressional committees – the Herter Subcommittee of the House Foreign Affairs Committee and the Smith-Mundt Congressional Group. Fortunately, for the future of the information program, 1947 was an off year in Congressional elections. Congressmen representing both committees had the time to visit foreign countries.

Reports from the returning Congressmen were not favorable – there was a deplorable state of misunderstanding and misrepresentation of the United States and its policies amongst foreign audiences.

Having visited twenty-two countries for their analysis, both groups believed that the enactment of a bill was necessary to establish mutual understanding between the United States and other nations. They found that while the Truman Doctrine had been enunciated, and the details of the Marshall Plan had been suggested, support for these two U.S. programs was not apparent.

In order to stimulate the necessary public support, the Congressmen suggested that these and various other U.S. policies be backed by overseas information and cultural activities.

By 1948, the Berlin blockade confirmed the need for increased American presence overseas. Early in the following year, Congress reauthorized these information and cultural activities with a legislative mandate called the Smith-Mundt Act of 1948 (Public Law 402). This Act gave the Office of International Information Educational Exchange (OIE) legal status, and the Voice of America legislative sanction, and gave the information program permanent status. The programs were put in service to promote mutual understanding between the United States and other countries.

By including a statute that barred the distribution of any of the agency's materials within the United States, the law helped to lessen the fear that USIA would become a domestic propaganda apparatus. The statute essentially prevented the U.S. government from becoming a government-run propaganda organization capable of propagandizing the American people. Any USIA product considered for distribution in the U.S. required an approval from Congress.

Radio: A Tool of Ideological Confrontation

In times of crisis, international radio broadcasting served as a major political tool in the ideological confrontation between the East and the West. During the early Cold War period, Soviet propaganda was at an all time high with the United States broadcasting counter-attacks via shortwave – each country vying for listeners and supporters in the cold-war ideological debate. The amount and intensity of radio broadcasting changed as regularly as crises and peace encroached on the international environment.

By 1950, the U.S. had awakened to the Soviet threat. The Soviets were tampering with foreign opinion to promote what one author described as "an international class community dedicated to the overthrow of established capitalistic governments."

In response, in June 1951, the United States Government established the Interdepartmental Psychological Strategy Board, which was accountable to the National Security Council in the Department of State. Using obsolete hot war communication techniques, the Psychological Strategy Board's mission was to plan and execute long-term approaches to national problems and, most importantly, to help influence opinions, attitudes, and behaviors abroad in support of U.S. objectives.

But, the Board's techniques simply did not work. Psychological techniques and methods using during wartime were no longer useful, nor were they necessary during the Cold War of words.

An outgrowth of the growing anti-communist sentiment used during the Cold War was President Truman's "Campaign of Truth," which followed the coup d'état in Czechoslovakia, the Soviet atomic bomb explosion, the Berlin blockade, and the defeat of the National forces in China. With a record appropriation of $121,000,000, this campaign was set up to expose the "big lie" techniques of the Soviets.

The onset of the Korean War underscored the need for more overseas information activities. Consequently, Congress tripled the funds for international information activities and increased the budget to $86 million, three times more than in 1948. Voice of America transmission facilities received much of the monies for major expansion of its shortwave transmitting capabilities. The Russians felt the stepped-up efforts and installed an electronic system to jam the Voice of America.

Investigations and Recommendations

In January 1953, four investigations of the U.S. information program were being conducted simultaneously by the Eisenhower Administration: 1) the Jackson Committee was established to clarify the function of the program; 2) two separate investigations conducted by the Senate, including the Hickenlooper Committee (Senator Bourke Hickenlooper, Chair), and the committee chaired by Senator Joseph McCarthy to clarify function, form, and purpose; and 3) the House of Representatives investigation conducted to determine program's finances.

The Jackson Committee (President's Committee on International Information Activities), headed by New York attorney William H. Jackson, examined, surveyed, and evaluated America's information program including covert activities, and paid particular reference to international relations and national security. In addition to studying the problem of psychological warfare, the committee also made recommendations for improvement of the U.S. government's information program.

The final report of the committee noted that American propaganda should be used to show and explain American goals by creating a positive climate of opinion necessary for accomplishment of U.S. policies. Other suggestions and conclusions of the Jackson Committee were to abolish the Psychological Strategy Board; focus on objective, factual news reporting; avoid propagandistic activities; use the information service for "forceful and factual refutations" to Soviet accusations; and create a climate of favorable opinion with truthful propaganda.

Following the committee's recommendations and responding to the poignant suggestion that the U.S. information program was confused about its mission, President Eisenhower removed the information function from the State Department with his Reorganization Plan #8, and on August 1, 1953, with the approval of the 83rd Congress, created the new and autonomous United States Information Agency (USIA). In the same year, the Voice of America was transferred to USIA and operations were moved from New York to Washington. News coverage focused on factual news and more features on U.S. developments.

Under the command of Theodore S. Streibert, a New York radio executive who was directly responsible to the President through the National Security Council, the new agency and its USIS centers and staff all over the world were sanctioned to submit evidence to peoples of other nations to show that the objectives and policies of the United States were in harmony with their legitimate aspirations for freedom, progress, and peace.

Independent of the State Department, but still under its policy control and guidance, USIA operated the Voice of America broadcasting service, an overseas public relations arm of the State, and a section focusing on cultural exchange.

Notably, the efforts of the Eisenhower administration's critique and appraisal of the information program, and the series of directives that emerged strengthened the agency's permanence. Official participation in the formulation and development of foreign policies became a reality.

From 1953 to 1960, the agency faced numerous problems ranging from unpopular directors and fluctuating appropriations to intense scrutiny from additional committees.

For example, after a lengthy investigation of the U.S. overseas information programs, the Senate Hickenlooper Committee noted that the objectives of the information program were not understood and that the "psychological strategy" of the United States was in bad shape. The Committee called the problem a matter of urgency.

Others submitted that the propaganda efforts had "gotten off on the wrong track" and "needed to be started all over again...(the U.S.) propaganda effort has been a spectacular flop from beginning to end."

Similarly, the 1953 Voorhees Report, written by the distinguished committee headed by former Congressman Tracy Voorhees, addressed the weaknesses of the information organization and concluded that the weaknesses resulted from numerous policy inconsistencies. The committee, which was formed to create a plan for an independent agency, also recommended a clarification of the agency's role in the foreign policy arena.

In the 1960s, President Kennedy struck a responsive chord in the American public with his vigorous attempt to respond to the threat of Communism. He created a new concern for the role of USIA and established numerous task forces to examine the agency's information and cultural programs.

In 1961, he gave the agency's newly appointed director, Edward R. Murrow assurances that the Kennedy administration would give the agency high priority. By 1963, the agency focused on influencing public attitudes. Though not sanctioned by Congress, the new mission statement of the Kennedy administration clarified and upgraded the role of USIA.

In 1965, Leonard Marks, a lawyer specializing in communication, was appointed USIA director. Operating under President Johnson's prescribed assumption that USIA had no propaganda to peddle, he created a new phase in the U.S. information program and called it "nation building." With a diminished emphasis on persuasion and propaganda, he focused on the sharing of information between countries to achieve mutual goals.

During the 1960s, U.S. radio output of the Voice of America, and the other government-financed radio services, namely Radio Free Europe and Radio Liberty expanded broadcasting in 18 languages – 168 hours per week in Russian, 91 in Ukrainian, and 63 in Byelorussian. Radio Free Europe broadcast to Bulgaria, Romania, Poland, and Czechoslovakia.

In August 1964, in response to the increased foreign broadcasting from Western nations, Radio Peace and Progress, a new service declared by the Soviets as independent and free from government influence, joined Radio Moscow in broadcasting from the Soviet Union.

Defaulting to a Strategy of Truth

During the two World Wars and the Cold War, achieving credibility was the major aim of U.S. and British propaganda. In 1918, Lord Northcliffe, Britain's head of the Ministry of Propaganda, made what some called a peculiar contribution to propaganda when he suggested that propaganda be truthful and linked to a definite policy. Adherence to truth made Northcliffe's propaganda keen-edged and deadly. The more truthful his war propaganda was, the more effective it was. Others who used false news, untruthfulness, or the suppression of truth during this time were usually not successful.

Allied propagandists, in general, tried to keep an essence of truth in their wartime messages. In the U.S., one of the first formal recommendations that propaganda be truthful came from the 1953 Presidential Committee on International Information Activities. The recommendation qualified President Eisenhower's October 1953 Statement of Mission for the United States Information Agency and established truth as a modus operandi.

Furthermore, U.S. policy makers believed that the U.S. information program should tell the truth to sell good will, and through this behavior extend a commitment to an open marketplace of ideas that would even feature both the diversity and the divisions of the American society.

After the two World Wars ended and as the Cold War subsided, distorting propaganda messages for some pre-determined reaction was not a practice used by U.S. information strategists. Unlike some of their predecessors who operated organizations that specialized in black propaganda (i.e., Office of Strategic Services), the new information corps of the United States Information Agency upheld the view that for a peaceful and enduring international order, messages to other parts of the world should be based on facts and not manipulation.

Policy makers reasoned that communicating factual and truthful information would create a climate of favorable opinion towards the U.S. They believed that factual and truthful information would stimulate reason.

Furthermore, they argued, if that information was judged as right and true by the audience, gaining that audience's assent would be easier. Factual and truthful information could support the communicators' intent to build credibility and authenticity and could possibly persuade the enemy to trust the messenger, even if that messenger was the enemy. U.S. sentiment was geared toward a straightforward presentation of truth to support a peaceful world order and an abandonment of propaganda that incorporated hard sell techniques.

CHAPTER FOUR

Public Diplomacy

Before World War I, foreign service officers formally carried out diplomacy through indirect communication with government officials, existing power structures and political elites to influence policy issues. Foreign service officers did not appeal directly to the public.

During World War I and II, the situation changed. Governments realized that dealing only with foreign governments and not foreign peoples was not in their best interest. Military prowess and the rhetoric of traditional diplomacy, which was relied on in the past, were being replaced by diplomatic activities involving the public.

Attitudes of peoples of other countries were important determinants of what a nation's foreign policy could accomplish.

Consequently, policymakers came to believe that traditional government-to-government diplomacy should be augmented with a government-to-people element.

The opinions, attitudes, and perceptions of citizens, who are also playing a more active role in government decision-making and influencing government policy making, have become important to policy makers in international affairs. They have realized that it is to their benefit to continue activities that inform public opinion and affect acceptance of U.S. policies.

The changing complexities of international relations forced the U.S. to use as many resources as possible to make diplomacy effective. The rapid advances in technology and the resulting information explosion contributed to this drastic metamorphosis in foreign relations and diplomacy. Radio broadcasting, satellite television broadcasting, and other secondary communication methods have supplemented the traditional channels of diplomacy, have facilitated increasing government-to-people interactions, and have made public diplomacy easy and convenient. These channels of communication gave nations a chance to affect an increasingly important world "public opinion."

Public diplomacy, which has become a viable and vital tool of statecraft, augments traditional diplomacy, assists in closing the understanding gap, and is evidence of traditional diplomacy's adaptation and evolution to the demands and pressures of modern mass communication and international affairs.

Public diplomacy materially affects and influences the formation of world opinions. It is the effort that a government makes to improve relations directly with the people of other countries. A complex and vital part of international relations, public diplomacy incorporates information activities, which are used for advocacy, and cultural activities, which serve a longer-term educational role in both the public and private domains.

People-to-People Element Increasing

Even though public diplomacy has been a discussed and debated subject for over four decades, it is still a relatively unexamined segment of international relations. As early as 1961 in a report by the Carnegie Endowment, the idea of public diplomacy was discussed, though the term was not used.

Describing the changing nature of diplomacy, the report noted that foreign activity (new diplomacy) was involving more people-to-people contact, and that in order to remain a world leader the United States should adopt new tools (e.g., information services, ministries of propaganda, and cultural activities) to respond to the stepped-up pace of diplomacy involving foreign publics.

Though the term had been used before to describe a broad set of activities involving the public, Edmund Guillion in 1965 coined the phrase public diplomacy to describe informational, educational, and cultural activities of the U.S. government, as well as non-governmental, private sector, and other "people" programs. It should also be noted that Whitton (1966) wrote of public diplomacy the same year that Guillion supposedly coined the phrase.

In an article likely submitted to the publishers in early 1965 and published in the spring of 1966, Whitton used the term public diplomacy. His definition, though, did not incorporate the tenets of Guillion's definition. He (Whitton) used the term to describe the airing of charges and opinions and ideas related to those charges in international assemblies or other public meetings...a place for relevant parties to make and fully defend accusations.

The Fletcher School of Law and Diplomacy, a graduate school in international relations, established the Edward R. Murrow Center for Public Diplomacy and created public diplomacy studies as an academic discipline – a field of specialized professional and academic status in the foreign relations community. Center professionals perceived diplomacy as encompassing the cause and effect of public attitudes and opinions that influenced the formulation and execution of foreign policies, and proposed to treat public diplomacy as a viable and developing dimension of international relations (Fisher, 1972).

Public diplomacy was seen as a complement to military and economic programs geared to fortifying the United States and as an investment in national security. Despite the disagreements on the definition of public diplomacy and an evident misunderstanding of the word, the literature supported the idea that public diplomacy was in fact essential to the security of the United States.

Over the years, the United States has underinvested in its public diplomacy efforts. For example, while the arsenals of defense are stocked with up-to-date weaponry such as the patriot missile (a weapon of the Strategic Defense Initiative), the United States has typically neglected the technology of broadcasting. In 1982, the Voice of America was using transmitters that were state-of-the-art in 1938, and there was a lack of continuous input of capital funds, particularly at a time when there had been numerous strategic developments in electronics. Because of this, the U.S. allegedly had lessened its capacity for world leadership and had diminished its prospects for security and well being.

USIA - The Public Diplomacy Agency

Conscious of public diplomacy challenges, the Reagan Administration made attempts to remedy the glaring deficiencies in the public diplomacy program conducted by the United States Information Agency. The Administration's political rhetoric led to increased funding.

In 1982, a House Foreign Affairs Committee report stressed the significance of public diplomacy and recommended increases in funding to assist the USIA in playing a stronger role in promoting national security and a more forceful role in the continuing war of ideas.

As America's public diplomacy agency established under the legislative mandate provided in the Smith-Mundt Act of 1948 and the Fulbright-Hays Act of 1961, the USIA made a concerted effort, albeit without the necessary funding and manpower, to increase mutual understanding of foreign peoples, and to utilize public diplomacy techniques and supporting technologies for more efficient global communication.

Pendulum-like swings in politicians' and policy makers' views and floating definitions of the agency's role adversely affected funding and performance. Despite this, a widespread view of many, at the time, was that USIA had come into its own, and the work it carried out under the vague, but useful term of public diplomacy would be even more important in the years ahead as citizens around the world played a greater role in influencing their governments' foreign policies.

Although it sometimes struggled to obtain a favorable hearing for American policies, one major victory USIA accomplished in its history was that "it had become the focal point for debate about its mission, its objectives, and its methods..." But, being the focal point for all of the debate certainly did not guarantee that its mission, objectives, and methods were accepted and understood.

In the 1986 House of Representatives hearings before the Subcommittee on International Operations of the Committee on Foreign Affairs ("Oversight of Public Diplomacy"), Dante Fascell concluded that while most accepted the idea that public diplomacy was important, there still existed members of Congress who either did not know what USIA was doing or harbored different views of the agency's mission despite the fact that the organization existed under a specific charter.

Public Diplomacy Strategies

Congress and the executive branch received their share of the criticism regarding their ability to prepare coherent plans in the area of public diplomacy. Oftentimes, the criticism was warranted. Many members of Congress who voted on the fate of USIA's funding often expressed dissatisfaction with the agency's performance, yet had no idea of what the agency's mission or what it was accomplishing.

The following dialogue about VOA between Congresswoman Helen S. Meyner, New Jersey, and Chair Dante Fascell during the hearings of the U.S. House of Representatives Subcommittee on International Operations, Committee on International Operations (95th Congress), serves as a typical example:

> *Mrs. Meyner: Yes, Mr. Chairman, it might be helpful, because I don't know much about what VOA does, to get some sort of idea—*
> *Mr. Fascell: Now is the time.*
> *Mrs. Meyner: Yes. Well, how much of it is music, entertainment? How much of it is straight news? I don't have information on that.*

Does this vary from country to country? How much are we doing in Africa at the moment?
Mr. Fascell: Why don't we ask USIA when they got here, (sic) (U.S. House, 1977).

Policy makers who appropriated money to the agency were frequently uninformed about the agency's operations. Similar evidence is found in the same hearings on public diplomacy when Representative Leo Ryan, California noted:

I don't know very much about USIA at all in comparison with what I probably should know as a member of this subcommittee, and I have been on the subcommittee now for four years...there should be people visiting me regularly to inform me of the successes and perhaps to diminish some of the failures (U.S. House, 1977, p. 79).

In the history of USIA and of the U.S. propaganda and information program in general, evidence continued to suggest Congressional members who appropriated funding to USIA knew very little about the agency's overall operations. One might surmise that a committee that knows very little about an agency, for whatever reason, is usually unlikely to properly fund that agency's operations.

Agency Reorganization

Throughout the years, considerable emphasis has been placed on the reorganization of USIA and its programs. To its detriment, USIA has been the most studied agency in the history of the U.S. government. During the past three decades more than 31 major studies have been conducted on U.S. government propaganda, information, and cultural programs. The suggestions offered by the various studies have ranged from a complete redefinition of the public diplomacy mission or reordering of agency's functions to moving USIA back to the State Department. One study, in particular, suggested a total revamping of the United States Information Agency's structure to reflect a separation of public diplomacy programs from educational and cultural programs. All of the studies (i.e., The Stanton Report, The Murphy Commission Report, the report by the General Accounting Office, Comptroller General's Report to Congress, the reports from the House Foreign Affairs Committee, among others) attempted to redefine the proper role of public diplomacy programs and attempted to provide the framework for carrying out those programs. The "tainted" information programs were considered propaganda, and therefore bad; culture was considered pure, and therefore good. For some, separation of the two functions was the only answer.

In the congressional hearings on "Public Diplomacy and the Future," policy makers addressed the questions of whether or not there was a need for USIA programs and activities, and whether or not there should be a consolidation of cultural affairs activities. As in previous formal studies of USIA, reorganizing public diplomacy efforts was a common theme addressed in this forum. Several participants testifying about the definitions, aims, and purposes of public diplomacy, criticized the opposing party's recommendations and begged support for their own recommendations. Members of the Stanton Panel criticized the General Accounting Office recommendations and vice versa. Frank Stanton, chair of the Stanton Commission, called the General Accounting Office's draft for agency reorganization disappointingly vague, suggested that it was merely a restatement of the status quo, and that it did not address the real needs of an agency that needed to be restructured.

In response to the accusations, Comptroller General Elmer Staats of the General Accounting Office argued that the Stanton Commission's report did not identify the defects in the quality and efficiency of the existing program, a key factor in justifying their suggested major reorganization. He maintained that major arguments of the Stanton Commission's recommendations lacked significant evidence, and that most of the charges lacked substantiation.

In the same hearings, Dante Fascell, chair of the Subcommittee on International Operations, lamented that only a few of the recommendations suggested in previous hearings on public diplomacy were ever implemented.

The Stanton Panel suggested that policy-related information programs, general information programs, and cultural programs should be moved from USIA to the State Department. This type of reorganization, which required housing an independent agency in an agency with less flexibility, would have lessened USIA's public aspects abroad and would have limited the less traditional approaches to foreign audiences.

Congressman Leo Ryan noted he saw no valid reason to "bury" USIA in the State Department. He suggested that he was not aware of a scandal, public outcry, or any kind of event which would have warranted such a change, and concluded that although he had some understanding of the Stanton Panel's recommendations and suggestions for reform, he did not understand the origins of those recommendations. He implied that they were the result of a hidden power struggle or bureaucratic fight. The dialogue between Mr. Leo Ryan and Mr. Earl Staats, the

Comptroller General of the United States, during the subcommittee hearings on the issue farther suggested the spuriousness of the Stanton proposal:

> *Mr. Ryan: Do you see any crushing, urgent need for significant reform or change? Does your agency see any – ? There is a proposal here, but, if there were no proposal, would you find this particular area such a can of worms you would be forced to say that something needs to be done?*
> *Mr. Staats: The answer is in the negative (Ryan, 1977, p. 23).*

Later in the hearings, Ryan asserted that most of the recommendations and suggestions made prior to 1977 concerning USIA dealt with specific internal and organization changes needed and not with what he called external ones. While substantial changes were taking place in the external political environment, the bureaucratic squabbles about USIA focused primarily on the internal environment of the organization and very few on how the agency would respond to the changes taking place around the world.

The restructuring of the organization based on political realities, such as the developing nations' need for natural resources or regional political powers coming of age, was not done. The hearing participants concluded that the U.S. was not doing the public diplomacy job as effectively as it could, that funding was not as high as it should be, and that reorganization was necessary for doing a better job. Fascell lamented that; overall, the recommendations still lacked a "fundamental policy decision within the U.S. government as to how best deal with the problem of public diplomacy."

Roth maintained that a thorough investigation of these and other related proposals indicated that an extensive amount of time, effort and financial resources were dedicated to developing many ideas, suggestions, recommendations, and ideas that were never developed or acted upon.

> ...(T)he innumerable studies and reports stand as sad road signs to a consensus that never took place. Despite the human effort and the wisdom they represent, the U.S. government was...unable to decide what it wanted from these programs and how they might best serve U.S. foreign policy aims (Roth, 1984, p. 359).

Funding History

Tackling the agency's internal problems, or responding to the program recommendations was difficult when the resources needed to operate the programs were not available. Over the years, USIA operations were undercapitalized in both absolute and relative terms, and because of severe budget cuts in some years, USIA had to eliminate a number of its operations.

In 1980, USIA was operating in real dollar terms with less than one-half the money that was available for the operations thirty years prior. Not even reaching the half way mark of that figure, the proposed budget for 1981 was $448 million. Operating at that level in 1990, the budget would be near one billion dollars. Overall, USIA resources declined steadily until 1983 when the Reagan Administration proposed and approved a large increase.

Charles Z. Wick's directorship was the funding exception. During his eight-year term as Director of USIA under Reagan, funding was higher. Congress approved substantial increases to USIA budget by more than 80 percent from $458 million to $837 million. This was the first time in sixteen years that the decline had been arrested, giving the agency the necessary means to conduct public diplomacy.

Competition for funds from a limited government budget, unplanned reductions in the budget, the waxing and waning of the budget, and inflation adversely affected USIA operations. It is heartening to those who believe in the importance of public diplomacy that the long-time "starvation diet" of the agency had been to some extent overcome, particularly at a time of great pressure to reduce federal spending.

Though funding levels increased periodically, the agency still operated at a substantially lower budget than it enjoyed in its peak post war year. Lewis (1977) suggested that the underfunding could be partially blamed on an intimidated executive branch and bureaucracy both reluctant to ask for the funds to carry out their objectives. He observed that the attitude on the usefulness of USIA varied from administration to administration and that the success of acquiring significant funding ultimately depended on the agency director's relationship with the President.

Richardson (1977) argued that the real problem was not funding, but the need for a substantive mission for the agency and the obvious "lack of any overall capacity to develop and follow strategies of communication in the world" (p. 145).

In a 1990 U.S. Advisory Commission on Public Diplomacy report, the same idea was stressed. No comprehensive and resourceful public diplomacy strategy had been developed to address the needs of the new opportunities in Eastern Europe and the rest of the world.

Similarly, to solve the problems of coordination, Hitchcock (1988) proposed that better interagency planning and closer cooperation with the private sector was needed, in addition to improved training, which he believed was more important than funding issues or reorganization issues.

CHAPTER FIVE

PR, TV & Policy Clarification

Though satellites were used to transmit programs internationally as early as 1964 by USIA, and in the 1970s for special event coverage, radio program relays, and for transmitting overseas a few television programs each year, the actual cost of satellite time precluded the agency from devoting its resources to a full-fledged, global television operation.

Worldnet emerged as the world's first state-of-the-art, government-owned satellite television network, specifically established as an adjunct to traditional diplomacy to tell America's story to the world. Satellite television was, in the agency's analysis, the best way to communicate to those foreign publics who increasingly turned to television as their primary source of information. The system, which linked the agency's Washington headquarters with U.S. embassies, posts, and cultural centers throughout the world, was set up primarily to bolster international support for America.

Responding to a Public Relations Problem

Worldnet was configured in November 1983 in response to an immense public relations problem surrounding the U.S. invasion of Grenada. Charles Z. Wick, USIA director, was in Europe when the invasion occurred, and he noticed increasing negative public sentiment regarding the U.S. action. He returned to USIA determined to right the situation by offering a detailed explanation and rationale behind the U.S. policy decision.

Informing Alvin Snyder, director of USIA television services of the situation, Wick explained that the United States' best allies were disgruntled about the Grenada situation. He commissioned Snyder to design a satellite-delivered service that would allow journalists the opportunity to question U.S. policy makers about the matter. Snyder explained:

> *Charlie came back from Europe struck by the region's negative reaction to the Grenada situation. He wanted the populace to make up their (sic) own minds on a story based on the facts...He wanted a big television conference by satellite with television reporters so that they could ask questions of policy makers involved in the decision (Snyder, 1990).*

Snyder directed the United States Information Service staff in five European cities to invite journalists to the embassies, and at the same time, USIA staff in Washington put together a panel to defend the U.S. interventionist position. The guests included

Jeane Kirkpatrick at the United Nations in New York; two State Department officials in Washington, Assistant Secretaries of State for Inter-American Affairs, L. Craig Johnstone and James H. Michael, both in Washington; and two Caribbean prime ministers, J.M.G. Tom Adams, Prime Minister of Barbados, and John Compton, Prime Minister of St. Lucia.

This interactive satellite television broadcast far outstripped USIA's expectations. Wick and his colleagues felt that they had created "one heck of a hook-up" and had stumbled on "something of great consequence" – a communication tool to clarify misconceptions and misunderstandings about a U.S. policy stance. The Administration's position on Grenada had been clarified by one interactive broadcast (November, 1983) via Worldnet and had done so with worldwide media attention.

Described as a novelty and a service that offered a special contribution to the international news landscape, Worldnet stimulated more media coverage for USIA than it had received in the previous 30 years of its existence, according to agency officials. Strategists noted that the innovative electronic public policy forum had upgraded USIA's image as purveyor of information overseas.

Increasing Foreign Understanding and Policy Support

The mission and goals for the Worldnet service were similar to the overall agency goals: to increase foreign understanding and support of U.S. policies; to promote foreign awareness of American society; and to counter false information about America. Two additional goals of the service included using interactive and passive satellite communication overseas and giving policy makers an opportunity to speak to foreign audiences.

The technical objectives for Worldnet focused primarily on network expansion: to equip all overseas posts with TVRO dishes; to lease satellite time at a reasonable rate for 24-hour coverage and to develop a worldwide network for instantaneous communication between Washington and overseas missions.

Government-Sponsored Satellite Programming

As global publics increasingly turned towards television for information, governments around the world recognized its importance as a tool of public diplomacy and were allocating resources to set up and maintain a global television structure.

In 1988, France was targeting Africa with satellite programming (to disseminate French culture); and a thrice-daily satellite news feed available to 18 countries in Africa (free of charge), and to Latin America, the Middle East and Asia (subscription basis).

At that time, Germany disseminated programming to over five million cable households in Western Europe and planned to distribute programming to Eastern Europe once satellite viewing and cable distribution made it possible. Deutsche Welle, a German short-wave broadcaster, also planned to get involved in satellite distribution.

The Italian government sent news and other types of programming to Latin America where RAI, the Italian government radio station, had set up a dubbing and regional distribution center. The local television station in Uruguay tapped the news feed from Rome via a donated TVRO dish.

During this period, Television Espanola, the Spanish government station, provided a feed via satellite to Latin America. In order to forge closer ties with its former colonies, the Spanish government has publicly announced its intention to increase its satellite television use.

Reports indicated that the former Soviet Union, in an apparent response to Worldnet, had experimented with electronic (audio only) dialogues. The United States Information Service post in Peru reported that the former Soviets had inquired about establishing a service similar to Worldnet (Bell, 1989).

Worldnet successfully wedded satellite technology to public diplomacy and provided a much-needed interactive element to public diplomacy. The service, with its two-way, interactive communication capabilities, was specifically designed as insiders noted to support American policy overseas and to assist in closing the broadcast gap between the United States and the Soviet Union.

Worldnet Interactives

For USIS officers in foreign posts, the interactives were useful in a variety of ways – the programs actually increased opportunities to make new contacts and strengthen old ones, and offered much needed background information on U.S. foreign policy. For many of the embassies, interactives created specifically in response to crisis situations (i.e., Grenada) were needed to clarify certain aspects of the U.S. foreign policy stance and to allay misunderstandings. Because of these needs, the two-way audio, one-way video interactive programs emerged as the cornerstone of the network's programming.

In early 1984, USIA considered using duplex satellite video and actually tested digital video compression techniques that permitted two-way video and two-way audio. The agency opted for the lowest cost transmission means – two-way audio and one-way video transmission – for its interactive programming.

Cleared for all broadcast and excerpting rights, the interactives offered interested parties an unprecedented degree of access to information about the United States. The interactive teleconferences served as a vehicle for live, frank, and unrehearsed exchanges with U.S. guests who were questioned by key foreign contacts. The format allowed foreign journalists to ask uncensored questions. This was a unique feature that set Worldnet apart from other sources of programming overseas.

Journalists used information from the interactives in news articles and commentaries, radio and television broadcasts, and various other special projects. Information from the interactives were obtained by actual attendance at the live interactive, from a broadcast quality videotape or audio tape provided by embassy staff, or by having direct access to the Worldnet feed via a closed circuit system (i.e., hotels or cable systems).

To facilitate an interactive, much coordination was required between the USIS staff abroad and USIA staff in Washington. The embassy staff supplied appropriate guest participants for the interactive, coordinated the related activities at the embassy, and established the necessary contacts with the local media.

USIA staff in Washington usually conducted the research and background work, managed the technical aspects of the network, and executed the program. Any proposed theme or subject matter for the interactive program was required to pass certain embassy criteria, clearances and approval.

The program topic, which was usually designed for widespread participation, also coincided with the embassy's country plan objectives. If the area staff established relevancy, Washington staff would develop the program topic, and guest experts were recommended and invited to participate in the interactive.

A USIA administrative staff person provided the necessary background and laid the groundwork for the program. An embassy staff person prepared and sent out the invitations to appropriate guests – usually influential media executives, government officials and academicians.

Lastly, the technical aspects of the production were prepared. Under normal circumstances, an interactive involving as many as six posts could be set up in two or three days. For a fast breaking news event, an interactive could be put together in less than 24 hours.

Forty-five minutes prior to the broadcast, the USIS staff tested the equipment to ensure that the telephone link-up was secure, that a strong and steady video signal was available, and that all other elements of the technical set-up were coordinated. Guests were required to arrive at the "studio" no later than one-half hour before airtime to familiarize themselves with the telephone conference microphones.

At the same time at USIA headquarters, the anchor of the interactive, the show's guests, and the various technical crews prepared for the program. With the director and appropriate technical crew, the program would begin. Both teams counted down the final minutes before the program opened with the familiar Worldnet logo and theme music. Guests were introduced, and the necessary background information and supporting video footage were supplied. Following this, the one-on-one questioning commenced.

Once a program was completed, USIS staff submitted a program evaluation cable to Washington answering such questions as:

- Was the topic appropriate?
- Was the subject what they had expected to discuss?
- Was the right expert chosen?
- Was simultaneous interpretation audible and adequate?
- Was time parceled out fairly?
- Were there any technical problems?
- What kind of press coverage was received? ("Worldnet, The first," 1989).

One eventful interactive between President Reagan, West German Chancellor Helmut Kohl in Athens, Greece, and three Columbia Space Shuttle astronauts utilized five satellites, thousands of miles of cables and hundreds of technicians including staff from AT&T, COMSAT, and CBS. In addition to the numerous video and audio circuits required, an encoder converted the SECAM signal to the American standard so that stations in the United States could retransmit the picture and sound.

The Atlantic Major One satellite linked the signal down to the COMSAT earth station that connected the land and microwave circuits to USIA. Pictures from Spacelab were sent to NASA's satellite and were received in White Sands, New Mexico, for a signal conversion that allowed stations to telecast the signal from space. The SATCOM Fl-R satellite intercepted the signal and relayed it to the Johnson Spaceflight Center. USIA-TV and the White House received the broadcast via a land circuit.

Then, pictures and sound from Spacelab were sent from the COMSAT earth station in Etam, West Virginia, and uplinked to INTELSAT Atlantic Primary Satellite. One signal went to London and one to Frankfurt, and was distributed by land circuits to U.S. diplomatic missions.

Italy's earth station in Fucino received another signal that was again converted to the European System for the U.S. embassy in Rome. Another converter at the same location was used to convert the signal back to the American standard. That signal was sent to Athens, Greece, so that Chancellor Kohl could see and hear the program. ("Worldnet expanding," 1986).

The hub of all of this activity was at the agency's Studio A Control Room that was equipped with nearly 200 switches, telephones, a character generator, and numerous television monitors at USIA headquarters in Washington where there was constant phone communication with the participating embassies.

Expanding Worldnet's Technical Infrastructure

In the early history of the establishment of Worldnet's multifaceted infrastructure, USIA television engineers gave no technical specifications. Posts purchased equipment without a concern for standardization.

Once regular, daily service began, the move towards standardization followed. The agency provided the embassies, posts, and cultural centers with standardized high-band equipment for making broadcast quality tapes, and provided standardized amplifiers, monitors, headsets, microphones, and telephone, and interface equipment.

Other equipment dispensed by USIA included the following: a TVRO satellite antenna mounted on a concrete base, a cable to connect the antenna to the control room, which housed a satellite receiver, an antenna tracking controller, monitors, and videotape recorders (usually 3/4 U-matic recorders, VHS, or Beta). If the recorders were not in the same format as the host country's recorders, a standards converter or transcoder was also provided.

Several embassies housed videotape editing system and low band VTRs for dubbing purposes.

For embassies with unreliable power sources, a power regulator was provided. Embassies used large monitors or video projection systems and custom-built Sony interactive audio equipment, in addition to a teleconferencing telephone for the interactive broadcasts ("Response," 1986).

Because no single worldwide color video broadcast standard existed, the translation of USIA programming through expensive conversion equipment was necessary. This conversion from one standard to another during interactives posed numerous logistical problems. Each time a picture was sent to a country that used a different standard, another costly conversion would take place.

Besides creating conversion challenges, some interactives required up to five satellites for completion – i.e., three Atlantic satellites, one Pacific satellite, and one Indian Ocean satellite. Oftentimes, signals were doublehopped – sent to one satellite, down to a ground station, then to a second satellite, which beamed the signal to the appropriate ground station ("USIA Worldnet," 1986).

Despite recurring technical obstacles, a large proportion of the interactives were of better than average technical quality. Most of the problems that were experienced occurred with the audio portion of the program. Some interactives had problems ranging from a complete or periodic loss of audio and video to sound distortion.

In one case, the technicians tried to provide additional microphones for the questioners and accidentally disconnected all of the lines. Additionally, numerous participants at the embassies created problems for the technicians by the placement of the microphones during the interactive.

Journalists contributed to the mayhem when they would run out of questions before the planned end of the hour-long broadcasts. Asking questions via satellite was a new experience for some of the journalists, and many were intimidated by the technology.

In the years following the first interactive, USIA network engineers put together an infrastructure of earth stations, satellite transponders, microwave links, and TVROs – a total 154 by 1989. The global network was able to transmit satellite programming and established a usage capability for audio support and a mechanism for forwarding government classified information to embassies.

This secondary feature helped to reduce the amount of money spent on telecommunication charges to receive the Wireless File – a USIA news and information service. Established in 1935 and originally used to send U.S. policy information (i.e., news, policy statements, background materials, and VOA commentaries) by teletype, the Wireless File service sent information to public affairs officers in 214 embassies and posts in five geographic regions via computer, landlines, and teletype in English, Spanish, French, and Arabic.

Contract Negotiations

USIA officials consulted senior Postal, Telephone, and Telegraph (PTT) officials from various countries to assess interest in Worldnet programming before opening competitive bidding amongst European PTTs in late 1984 for Worldnet's proposed five-day-per-week feed to Europe. France DGT, the French PTT service, won the contract. A $1.6 million accord was signed. The turnkey contract included terms for leasing a French transponder that enabled USIA to transmit programming to Eastern and Western Europe.

With the signing of this contract, the cost of a one-hour Worldnet transmission to Europe was reduced by 90% – from $35,000 to $3,000.

In addition to pursuing contract negotiations for lower transmission costs in overseas markets, USIA actively solicited free television materials from independent television stations, independent producers, networks, commercial sources, associations (i.e., the U.S. Chamber of Commerce), and ideas and information from medical, and technical and scientific experts in the United States. Numerous media organizations also supplied free programming to USIA.

By mid-October 1984, some 19 hours of material broadcast by ABC, CBS, NBC, and PBS was obtained for servicing requests from 14 posts...CBS and NBC permitted USIA to offer *Face the Nation* and *Meet the Press*, respectively, to posts worldwide for in-house use at no cost, while William F. Buckley, Jr. and Producers, Inc. gave the agency worldwide in-house rights to the PBS show *Firing Line* at no cost.

Additionally, in late 1985, Post Newsweek offered *Agronsky and Company*, the weekly public affairs discussion show for closed circuit use. A similar program, already on the network and also offered free to Worldnet, was *The McLaughlin Group*.

Faced with a shrinking budget, USIA also opted to enlist the help of Fortune 500 companies such as DuPont, Kodak, Ford, Boeing, IBM, and United Technologies. Through these contributions, Worldnet programming costs were significantly reduced ("USIA Worldnet," 1986).

Growth of Worldnet Programming

During its first full year of operation, Worldnet offered cable subscribers throughout Europe over 520 hours of programming – two hours per day, five days per week. The COMSAT Atlantic Satellite beamed a signal to a station near Paris that redistributed it over the continent.

Worldnet's popularity and growth in Europe coincided with the increasing acceptance of cable television by European PTTs, so "selling" free programming to start-up operations was not a difficult task. New cable outlets searched for interesting and informative programs to fill their extensive programming needs.

At that time, a varied and steady supply of programs was not available to the European cable systems, hence the burgeoning cable industry created a need for programming. Worldnet was available to fulfill part of that need.

Wick reported that USIA received numerous unsolicited inquiries about the Worldnet service. Trying to pave the way for more cable negotiations, he instructed USIS officers overseas to solicit other cable companies and hotels and inquire about the institutions, possible interest in carrying the Worldnet signal.

For a cable network, it was easy to take Worldnet on board. It carried no advertising (which might infringe on local or national regulations), and it was completely free of charge. Moreover, its transmission hours...made it entirely suitable for channel sharing. The channel was transmitted in the clear, was not encrypted, and was fully available for dish-owners to pull down its signal without payment.

While Wick was negotiating lower transmission costs and permission to air agreements, funding for Worldnet continued to increase, and Worldnet's transmission schedule continued to expand. For fiscal year 1985, the network received approximately $13.9 million, including $11 million for satellite transmission. In 1985, the agency also requested, in 1985, $22,264,541 to support a daily broadcast schedule, which included documentary films, English language training, classic American feature films, sports coverage, business, science, and entertainment news.

Passive Programming

Initiated in April 1985 after the finalization of USIA/French PTT agreement for 10 hours of transponder time per week, Worldnet's passive programming was set up as a secondary delivery system for the U.S. government – non-broadcast system which used CATV or host country PTTs to either rebroadcast or air on a delayed basis. April 22, 1985, marked the first daily transmission of passive Worldnet programming, and the U.S. government became the first government to operate a daily international television service. The schedule was two hours per day, Monday through Friday.

Differentiating between these types of distinctly different programming was necessary when describing the Worldnet service. As the history of the network unfolded, critics focused not on the network as an entity, but more specifically on the attributes and characteristics of the two types of programming. The news and entertainment portions (passive program offerings) included *America Today*, a live, hour-long, talk-show format program with briskly paced news stories, showcases of members of Congress, scientists, and journalists; and live remote broadcasts, as well as videotaped reports.

Satellite File, a weekly half-hour news program similar to *America Today*, was described as USIA's most watched, most successful program worldwide. Seen in over 95 countries, the program was offered in English, French, Arabic, and Portuguese, and it highlighted American life, current events, news background, and information on the cultural heritage of the United States.

This particular program was provided free of charge to news organizations, such as VISNEWS which had clients in 86 countries and UPI-TN which had 30 clients in 26 countries. Used extensively for taped relay in universities and schools, *Science World*, a weekly science digest program, highlighted all fields of scientific achievement – i.e., discoveries and scientific innovations including medical developments, and discovery of new objects in the universe (Fortune 500 companies provided material for this program free of charge).

Another talk show format program, *Almanac*, featured both celebrity guests and guests who were considered average American citizens. The subjects ranged from world hunger to education.

By January 1985, large audience segments were reached by Worldnet via Eutelsat's new European Communication Satellite (ECS-1), which provided overlapping spot beams for cable systems to receive Worldnet programming free and to TVRO dishes at 60 American embassies and consulates in Europe and Scandinavia, and to numerous cable networks and hotels.

Congressional Delegation

As Worldnet expanded its reach, policy makers became concerned about its impact and influence. Three years in operation, the service's overseas impact, both on foreign publics and on embassy personnel, had not been analyzed. A congressional staff delegation was organized to do just that.

Those participating in the seven-day project, conducted the week of January 12-18, 1986, were: Richard McBride, Staff Director, House Subcommittee on International Operations; Susan Andross, Staff Consultant and Ken Peel, Minority Staff Consultant, House Subcommittee on International Operations for Olympia Snowe, ranking minority member of the Subcommittee; Thomas Harvey, General Counsel, USIA; and Bruce Gregory, Staff Director, United States Advisory Commission on Public Diplomacy.

The group visited several major cities to find out if Worldnet programming reached the opinion makers and the mass audience, what type of programs were successful, and how embassy personnel adjusted to the new responsibilities associated with the service. The delegation chose three foreign capitals receiving the Worldnet service to undergo the extensive investigations: London, Paris, and Brussels. Though the broadcast regimes of the relevant nations were different, equipment and theatre facilities were available at the U.S. embassies located in each of these cities.

The group spent two days in each location to analyze the Worldnet operations, review audience claims, talk to opinion makers, find out why certain programs were or were not successful, look at the impact of the increased workload at the embassies, and analyze field reactions of foreigners who participated in the Worldnet dialogues (McBride, 1992).

According to McBride, overseas investigatory work was frequently conducted by delegations made up of congressional staffers instead of congressmen. He commented that congressmen rarely conducted investigations like this: "It's better to go without them anyway. They find this kind of detail work boring and a waste of their time."

McBride explained that even without congressmen, a concerted effort was made to include the "right people" in the group.

Since Worldnet was the brainchild of Charles Wick, we felt safe inviting someone – Thomas Harvey – from his camp. He reported directly to Wick. If we considered saying anything negative about the broadcast, whether irrelevant or not, we had better have some evidence to support our claims. What better way to accomplish a balanced report then to have USIA General Counsel and the Staff Director of the U.S. Advisory Commission on Public Diplomacy at all of the meetings. By the time the process had been completed, all of us agreed on the recommendations that were put in the report. As you might imagine, Wick didn't like it. We hoped that he wouldn't kill the messenger. Well, he blew up. He didn't want anyone criticizing Worldnet. All in all, I believe that the recommendations we made were constructive, but I don't believe Wick viewed them that way (McBride, 1992).

At all three post locations, the delegation visited the U.S. ambassador, members of the local press, including Worldnet Dialogue participants, cable television owners and operators, and government officials responsible for broadcasting and telecommunication policy. In London, the group found:

- A competitive and well-developed national news industry which successfully fulfilled Britain's need for news and information
- Many barriers to USIA's establishment of a market for the official policy pronouncements on Worldnet
- A certain amount of pressure had been put on U.S. embassy staff by USIA in Washington to participate in interactives and to direct the subsequent placement of Worldnet news in local press and television
- Dwindling staff resources had been used to obtain journalists, who many called the interactives "fake news conferences" and often complained that the comments of the particular U.S. government officials were irrelevant, not newsworthy or timely, and that these same officials could be interviewed in Washington by the respective foreign correspondents ("Response," 1986).

The environment in France was somewhat different. Politically sensitive to foreign broadcasts and operating in an uncertain broadcasting regulatory environment, the French government closely supervised French television and generally placed numerous restrictions on broadcasting. But surprisingly, the government's regulations for the cable industry were not as stringent. In fact, at that time, the industry was in a state of flux and provided Worldnet an opportunity to supply programming.

Overall, French attitudes towards Worldnet were positive. Embassy officials in Paris supported Worldnet and noted that its timing was perfect. The Public Affairs Officer (PAO) agreed with Director Wick's view that Worldnet was a good way to get the U.S. international broadcasting effort started before governments and international regulatory organizations set up rules and regulations to prevent such a service. The PAO also said Worldnet was a useful tool when he needed to clarify certain aspects of U.S. policy and added that the explanatory role was its most important attribute.

The delegation's report suggested that the Worldnet network was popular in Belgium primarily because of the fascination with the new technology – the medium used to deliver the story was the story. In that country, Worldnet interactives were held in a spacious American Cultural Center, instead of the usual cramped quarters of an embassy.

Worldnet gave the foreign journalists there a chance to obtain access to foreign policy decision makers and spokespersons. In a casual and non-intimidating atmosphere, the journalists had direct access to that individual, and did not have to compete with the "aggressive" U.S. press corps for information.

U.S. Ambassador Geoffrey Swaebe in Brussels was enthusiastic about Worldnet and praised the service for giving him an opportunity to follow the news, for helping the embassy to increase contacts, and for aiding the embassy in combatting misinformation put out by other governments. Ambassador Swaebe also detailed the service's faults, noting that the daily product quality was often lacking. He concluded that the service was valuable only if it were cost-effective, reached the right market, and was a good product.

In general, the most common complaint offered by all three posts was that if an interactive was cancelled at the last minute, it seriously affected the credibility of the USIS officers involved. The most significant conclusion of the delegation was that interactives were a useful part of the Worldnet service, and passive programming did not seem to be serving any functional or practical purpose. The group also expressed doubts that the passive type of programming should be broadcast at all.

Network and Budget Expansion

The growth of the network was not without incident. Though many cable systems and hotel chains accepted Worldnet programming – the agency reported that 3.7 million cable subscribers received Worldnet and over 25 hotels in Europe carried the signal via rooftop dishes – numerous systems and organizations turned down Worldnet's offer for free programming. For example, the European Broadcasting Union, a clearinghouse for international news film and reporting, turned down a trial tape that was offered to them, noting that Worldnet footage was used only when the organization was unable to locate footage from another source.

During the early years of the Reagan presidency, agency activities took an almost combative tone and reflected the Administration's view that the Cold War still existed. Both Soviet and American officials saw each others' propaganda efforts as an extension of war efforts – a Cold War which focused on the minds of men – a type of ideological warfare. Each country was enamored with the illusion that "anti" attitudes had some relevance and supported the rationale for stepped-up information activities.

The statement that the Russians were outspending the Americans in propaganda legitimized expenditures in information. Oftentimes, U.S. officials quoted figures on Soviet information expenditures for comparison with the paltry amount spent by the U.S. government. They rationalized that U.S.

spending was not high enough and pushed for greater funding for U.S. information efforts.

Soviet officials attributed a comparable notion to U.S. official's efforts and described Worldnet as an instrument used for the interference of a state's internal affairs. But despite the initial reservations about Worldnet as an instrument of propaganda, in the end, the Soviets cooperated in numerous ventures with USIA and Worldnet staff.

In 1986, the agency budget grew to $837 million, and by 1987, USIA requested $959 million. Wick requested the nearly $1 billion from the U.S. Congress to counter what he called "sophisticated and determined efforts of the Soviets" who were trying to influence public opinion worldwide. The bulk of the money went towards upgrading technical capabilities, bolstering longstanding programs, and experimenting with new ways of communicating.

In April 1987, the broadcast day to the European network was doubled from two to four hours daily, and the number of interactive programs, officially called Dialogues, was up to 289. Additionally, Worldnet developed two new programs specifically for Latin America. One of the programs, *Calidoscopio Semanan*, a one-half-hour magazine format show, featured Latino achievements in the arts and industry. Also in 1987, with the addition of the U.S. mission in West Berlin and the embassy in Guadalajara, Mexico, one third of the 160 high priority sites were receiving Worldnet.

Evaluation of the Worldnet Service

In December 1987, the U.S. Congress passed legislation to severely limit the Worldnet service. In that authorization bill,

Senate Foreign Relations Committee Chairman Claiborne Pell (D-R.I.) inserted a provision which required USIA to pull Worldnet's daily passive programs off the air after October 1, 1988, unless a congressionally-mandated survey of 11 European countries, including Belgium, Denmark, Finland, France, Federal Republic of Germany, Italy, Luxembourg, Norway, Sweden, Switzerland, and United Kingdom, found a minimum daily audience in Europe of at least 2 million.

In PL 100-204, Section 209, Pell's provision stated specifically that "(n)o funds authorized to be appropriated to the United States Information Agency shall be expended after October 1, 1988, or the production or acquisition of passive (non-interactive) programs for USIA's Worldnet television service unless...the survey show(ed) with a high degree of reliability that the average daily European audience for the passive (non-interactive) programs of USIA's Worldnet television service is not less than 2,000,000 viewers" ("Worldnet viewership," 1989).

Peter Galbraith, son of the famed economist, John Kenneth Galbraith and influential aide to Chairman Pell of the Senate Foreign Relations Committee, and the person who suggested the threshold figure of two million, remarked that there was not sufficient justification for an experimental project such as Worldnet. He explained that the service should not receive such a high level of funding at a time when budgets throughout the government were being reduced.

As a self-proclaimed watch-dog of USIA, he rationalized that with only a limited amount of money for operations, the agency was foolish to spend thirty or forty million dollars on a project which did not modernize American efforts overseas (i.e., VOA).

He added that USIA should spend the money on the VOA in order to broadcast a better signal for more hours.

Bill Eames, Assistant Director of Worldnet, suggested that one of the reasons for the reduced funding and the congressionally mandated survey was the result of a congressional dislike of the pace of television (Worldnet) expansion.

Others suggested that the creation of the congressional mandate was the result of negative reaction to the general overstatement of the case for television and the overuse of inaccurate language used to describe viewership patterns and audience totals. Bruce added that Worldnet's growth was not properly monitored.

What happened between, 83 and 87 was it (Worldnet) just grew by leaps and bounds...but it grew haphazardly, without any resistance. One detriment of the whole process was that it was a one-man shop – he (Wick) was running this thing out of his hip pocket...(he) did not want to accept any restrictions. He (Wick) wanted it carte blanche. He had the impression: "Don't get in my way. Give me the money I want, and if you don't give me the money, I am gonna take it from...the VOA...PAO staffs, etc. I am going to run this thing, okay." (Bruce, 1990).

The general overstatement of the need for international television, and inaccurate language used to describe viewership patterns and audience totals created an environment ripe for criticism and analysis from outsiders, including members of Congress who objected to its cost, believed few people were watching, and who were not fully convinced of the network's success. Others suggested that the mandate was politically motivated and was created as a result of the numerous personality conflicts between congressional staff members and Charles Wick.

McBride agreed that Worldnet was not on the Senate Foreign Relations Committee's favored program list.

> ...(the) Committee believed that broadcasting was a waste of money. The Committee favored putting more money into exchange programs. They took the constructive criticisms of Worldnet and turned them around to have an excuse to hold funding down. One person affected that committee. A senior staff person was able to convince the Chairman of the Committee that this was what they should be doing (McBride, 1992).

In a personal interview with Wick, he agreed with McBride and suggested that the survey and the arbitrary threshold set by Senator Pell's office was a "cynical hatchet attempt to kill something without addressing its merits," noting that the authorization bill was tampering with freedom of expression and freedom of information.

Similarly, in a letter to Senator Pell, Senator Howell Heflin (AL) inquired about the specific reasons for the use of the two million average daily viewers in Europe and wanted to know about the "reasoning for using only Europe as the base for the study."

Wick and others expressed the same concerns. Defenders of Worldnet argued that the requirement that Worldnet reach two million viewers among the European audience, therefore, appeared inappropriate and certainly should not have been the sole criterion on which the survival of the entire worldwide daily program service depended (Wick, 1988).

Peter Galbraith, who managed the authorization bill, explained that the two million threshold was based on Wick's declaration that the Worldnet audience far exceeded that number. In a personal interview, Eames offered his recollections about the matter:

Oh, the two million was a frivolous number. It was devised by Peter Galbraith. Peter has some strong views that Senator Pell agreed to. And, he did not believe that the U.S. government should be involved in sending out information at all...that the private sector television networks, including Cable News Network (CNN) were adequate for doing the job. Because not too many people were watching, he was able to put this bubble over on us. I asked him once: Where did you come up with that 2 million figure? And he said, "I took it out of my head. It is just as reliable a figure as the four billion that I heard Charlie Wick utter once. Mr. Wick was interviewed on a television program once and he said, 'oh, about billion.' Where he got four billion, God only knows. He always tried to make impressions. But anyway, he said four billion." Galbraith said that his two million looks just as good. He said to me, "I frankly didn't think you'd get more than two thousand in the survey, so, you are doing ten times better than I thought with twenty thousand. But you are ten times worse than you were supposed to be (Eames, 1990).

Sherwood Demitz, Chief of the Office of Media Research, in USIA's Office of Research in Washington, agreed that the two million threshold was artificially high and was not a realistic target for Worldnet.

Prior to the actual survey done by Burke-Inter/View of Amsterdam, Demitz conducted an analysis for the Worldnet service comparing audience figures of the mass entertainment channels, Sky Channel and Super Channel. Demitz tried to project what audience figures could reasonably be expected from a government-sponsored, narrowly focused news/public information service such as Worldnet, which broadcast during the midafternoon for only two hours per day. He concluded that, by definition, it was not possible for the network to garner an audience anywhere near 2 million people (Demitz, 1990).

When asked about Wick's downfall in the matter, Demitz cited that it was his imprecise use of audience survey terminology. He explained that Wick's statements progressed from "Worldnet is connected to a certain number of homes" to "Worldnet can be seen by a certain number of homes" to "Worldnet is seen by a certain number of people."

In a personal interview, Bruce (1990) confirmed Demitz's explanation and maintained that Wick's use or misuse of terminology also directly affected how others perceived the operation.

He (Wick) went so far as to say that the potential audience of Worldnet in 1985 or 1986 was five billion people. Now, there are only five billion people in the world. I don't care how you cumulate the numbers, even if you cumulate the numbers. How do you get five billion people? It's absurd. And the "five billion" epitomized the intensity with which he forced this thing to grow. He impinged on other territories, and that's where the bureaucratic turf fighting began...Then the preposterous claims started becoming louder and louder. That's when we got to the really ironic end to their passive programming. We said, okay, two million people in Europe or nothing...It sounds like two million came from nowhere...I suppose it came from the ten percent of the European audience Wick claimed (20 million)...they were serving him his own letter in fact. And in political terms, sometimes that's a necessary process (Bruce, 1990).

Wick staunchly countered the claim that the audience figures were fiction or inflated estimates and said that the allegations were without foundation. The numbers were based on data submitted by posts overseas – the best estimates of the available audience. Those figures, according to Wick, were totaled and that number was then used to describe the audience of Worldnet. The whole process was not meant to reflect precise statistical analyses, he added. The "ballpark" figures supplied by the embassies reflected possible audiences.

McBride suggested that Wick was merely attempting to provide a summary figure to show how Worldnet was doing – "a figure to use in his PR letters to Worldnet guests and to Congress." He implied there was not an attempt on the part of Wick to mislead.

> *Wick's numbers were not fabricated or made up, but they were meaningless. He was using a construct and statistics that made no sense. He got the information from PAOs who were instructed to find out how Worldnet was used. Then, he would add audience figures and circulation figures together. After each Worldnet, a cumulative total was presented. He should have somehow buffered what they were saying. In private meetings, we told Wick that it wasn't necessary to make flashy statements. It gave the members of Congress something to criticize. After these private meetings, the concentration was focused less on the audience figures (McBride, 1992).*

Audience Methods

USIA did use various "methods" of acquiring and cumulating audience figures. Supplied via cable by embassy Public Affairs Officers who monitored local media use of Worldnet, the figures were derived from newspaper circulation totals which were usually provided by the newspapers themselves, estimations of nightly audiences based on the participating television stations' estimates, audience surveys in various countries conducted by second parties, radio surveys of listenership, estimations of total television or radio sets in a given country, and press readership figures.

From these cables, Wick's staff derived estimated audience figures. The total of these numbers reflected a "gross average audience" for a particular broadcast. Further, in order to come up with what the agency called the "cumulative impact" of Worldnet, the analysts would add the gross average audience of Worldnet programs over a period of time. One figure – the cumulative audience reported at 4.1 billion – was derived by adding all of the reported gross average audiences for each program aired since the network began ("Worldnet: February," 1987).

In general, the methodology used to obtain the audience figures and the way these audience figures were described seemed to confuse not only Congressional staff, but also Director Wick. He failed to consider the obvious limitations and fallacies of the number accumulation and focused instead on unabashedly selling the network. His strong language coupled with the astonishing audience figures, had a negative effect on Congressmen who responded with Public Law 100-204. The fate of Worldnet passive programming rested on the results of the required European audience survey.

1988 – An Historic Year for Worldnet

All in all, 1988 was an historic year for the United States Information Agency and for Worldnet. The network celebrated its fifth anniversary. The technical infrastructure of Worldnet spanned the globe with a completed regional network system (EURONET, AFNET, ARNET, NEANET, and EANET).

The network began transmission on INTELSAT'S Indian Ocean Regional Satellite then later added the Near Eastern and Asian networks; conducted over 1,044 Dialogue interview programs; and completed a system which offered programming to 100 countries on six continents via cable, closed circuit, or broadcast through satellite links (Kline, 1988c).

Most importantly though, in August 1988, the results of the audience survey were published. The 11 European countries surveyed did not have the required minimum audience of at least 2 million.

Conducted in June 1988 by Burke-Inter/View of Amsterdam, The Netherlands, the television audience survey found that Worldnet passive programming garnered a pan-European cumulative audience of 234,262, 48% of the Worldnet universe on a daily basis and 1.33% of the Worldnet audience on a weekly basis.

In a personal interview, Chief of USIA Office of Research, Communications Media Branch, Sherwood Demitz explained that while the study did provide specific audience figures, the survey:

...did very little to produce any information that we did not already know. Nor did it produce any information that could help us to improve the quality of the product. Nonetheless, we tried to use it in a way that would benefit the agency by incorporating questions that would provide us with some viewer feedback for the readjustment of programs. All in all, the survey turned into a reasonably sophisticated instrument – a beautifully done survey research operation that was reasonably priced. Additionally, it was a tremendous undertaking.

The geographic scope was 11 countries. It was a tragedy that the unrealistic threshold wasn't met (Demitz, 1990).

On October 1, 1988, as required by Public Law 100-204, USIA cancelled all of Worldnet's passive programming. Exchanging some of its ideas about the survey with Congress in a document titled *Worldnet Viewership Around the World*, USIA noted that the Worldnet service was never intended to be strictly a European program and suggested that Worldnet's greatest impact would be on the Third World.

The report also cited the shortsightedness of Congress in not considering types of information crucial to evaluating the effectiveness of Worldnet, such as data about Worldnet viewership in other countries throughout the world. USIA added that "...no satellite delivered television service can presently hope to achieve 2 million daily adult viewers in the European market." Worldnet, with 234,262 mid-afternoon viewers, compared favorably with other satellite-delivered programs in Europe.

Restricted by the Congressional information embargo from airing passive programming, Worldnet staff continued to produce interactives. For example, the staff co-produced an interactive with Gosteleradio Radio in Russia that featured the Librarian of Congress Emeritus Daniel Boorstin and Russian professional peers discussing the preservation of national heritages.

This bilingual telebridge was transmitted live to Worldnet audiences on five continents, and Soviet television aired the program during prime time to an estimated 100 million viewers ("Worldnet: The first," 1989).

USIA continued to negotiate program agreements for the reduced-service Worldnet. On November 9, 1988, the agency signed an agreement with C-Span to transmit the network's public affairs programming.

Worldnet's technical expansion also continued. In 1989, USIA negotiated extended service on the EMBRATEL satellite for 24-hour access to Latin America, South America, and the Caribbean. With this development, Worldnet was available to 106 countries. By the end of fiscal year 1990, the agency had reached its goal of outfitting 100 percent of its 150 priority sites throughout the world.

During the last few months of 1988, the House passed legislation twice for Worldnet to resume daily service, but both attempts failed to get through the Senate. The action taken by Congress to interrupt passive programming service remained in effect until the 101st Congress.

CHAPTER SIX

Charlie Z. Wick

Known to Clevelanders as Charlie Zwick, former musician and 1940s band leader, Wick was actively involved in the financing and operation of several businesses in the health care and mortgage industries. Wick was a non-practicing lawyer whose first degree was in music from the University of Michigan. While in law school at Case Western Reserve University (formerly Western Reserve University) completing his law degree, Wick worked for Tommy Dorsey and Fred Waring bands. In later years, one of his production companies produced *Snow White and the Three Stooges.*

As a USIA director who served longer than anyone in the agency's 35-year history, Charles Z. Wick was once described by Ambassador Richard Burt, West Germany, as the person who made "communications technology the handmaiden of public diplomacy." Wick defined his role as director of USIA solely in terms of results and was enthusiastic about his ability to push projects through a sluggish bureaucracy. Nonetheless, Wick was fraught with critics who made public comments about his penchant for pageantry, lack of a background in world affairs, and lack of sophistication.

Agency employees expressed concern about his naive and dangerous Cold War rhetoric, his emphasis on USIA's potential as an anti-Soviet propaganda tool, his aggressive personality, his short fuse, and frequent outbursts of temper. Some called him a "strutting dictator" who needed media effectiveness training.

As described in the press, Wick imbued a personal style that was arrogant, flashy, and irrepressible. Wick did not help matters when he proclaimed early in his tenure that while he was not a newspaperman and didn't know anything about journalism or foreign policy, he did know how to make things happen (Goshko, 1986).

Rarely had a public official's personal style and directorship been so carefully scrutinized; but rarely did an agency have a director who had been as controversial. For example, during a meeting of the California Press Association, Wick told newspaper publishers that the British Prime Minister "opposed the invasion of Grenada because she is a woman." Reaction to this statement included eighteen U.S. representatives calling for Wick's resignation (Southerland, 1984).

Wick was also in the headlines more than any other director. Besides the numerous stories about his convoluted audience figures for Worldnet, he was accused of secretly taping telephone calls, installing a security system at his residence at government expense, authorizing a blacklist of speakers for USIA speaker's program, which included Walter Cronkite, and hiring relatives of friends and political connections.

Speculating that he may be a target of the KGB, Wick installed a $32,000 security system at his home initially at the government's expense. White House aides convinced him to reimburse the government in an effort to save the President from possible embarrassment.

Wick and the Secret Recordings

Within months of his arrival in Washington, he achieved notoriety both in the capital and the country at large. His directorship was riddled with problems and conflict including four separate probes for the surreptitious telephone taping (the State of Florida, the General Services Administration, the Senate Foreign Relations Committee, and the House Foreign Affairs Committee). Each group investigated the legal and ethical implications of Wick's secret tape recordings.

When he was first confronted about the tapings, he denied them. Top-level agency sources said that the practice had been going on for some time and that Wick had been cautioned on numerous occasions in a memorandum from USIA General Counsel.

After initial denials, Wick presented USIA with transcripts of telephone conversations with several individuals – Senator Mark Hatfield, R-Oregon, Chairman of the Senate Appropriations Committee; Kenneth Adelman, Director of the United States Arms Control and Disarmament Agency; Geoffrey Swaebe, U.S. Ambassador to Belgium; Walter H. Annenberg, former ambassador to Great Britain; and several others – who later admitted that they had no knowledge their conversations with Wick were being taped.

After it was made known that he had taped telephone conversations surreptitiously, Wick finally admitted that he had taped some of his conversations, but added that the nonconsensual taping and transcribing were used as a management tool to "ensure appropriate follow-up on any action items and other matters of concern."

According to the GSA report that detailed Wick's taping activities, Wick had been informed as early as 1981 by two agency employees of the propriety of this kind of practice. Executive Assistant Robert Earle and former Deputy Director Gilbert A. Robinson expressed similar dissatisfaction with the practice. Robinson was later fired from USIA by Wick for his role in hiring and promoting efforts in USIA "Kiddiegate" scandal.

The report substantiated the fact that a memo and a copy of the relevant GSA regulations were forwarded to Wick on or about December 17, 1981, from USIA General Counsel Jonathan W. Sloat detailing the acceptable federal procedures (i.e., obtaining prior consent for all parties for each conversation).

Wick issued a statement of apology to domestic and overseas agency employees that said that while the practice of recording a telephone conversation was not illegal, others might construe the practice as intrusive. Wick believed that since the GSA regulations did not establish specific sanctions if breached, he could continue the practice without fear of legal obstacles, but decided that it was in his best interest to end the practice.

He remarked that the recordings, which were done simply to help him extend the reach of his memory, was a major political blunder and wrote over 120 letters and made calls of apology to each of the persons he taped. He blamed the initial denials and misinformation on his own anxiety about the matter and his faulty recollection. He further added that he meant no offense to anyone.

Despite the unusual public condemnation for the incidences, including comments from White House Chief of Staff James Baker III who was taped during one of his conversations with Wick, there was no evidence that White House officials were pressing for Wick's dismissal. His firing was not expected.

In fact, President Reagan expressed confidence in Wick throughout the ordeal. In an attempt to squelch additional rumors that Wick would resign, President Reagan spoke out for Wick, praised his performance, and reemphasized that he would remain as chief of USIA.

White House Counselor Edwin W. Meese III echoed the president's public vote of confidence, saying it was his belief that Wick did not see the practice as unethical and that it was a business practice he carried with him from his previous private sector activities.

The Kiddiegate Scandal

Another major investigation by the General Accounting Office (GAO) involving Wick and USIA was focused on his much-criticized hiring practices, "including his record of peppering USIA payroll with Hollywood cronies and relatives of high-ranking officials in the Reagan administration." GAO and two congressional committees were responding to complaints from the American Federation of Government Employees that children of several prominent administration officials had received preferred USIA career jobs.

Wick and his staff hired roughly 150 persons with political connections, and according to the GAO report, included immediate relatives of presidential appointees, and among the hirings reported in the press were Wick's piano teacher, and the widow of General Omar Bradley.

A few of the employees hired during the Kiddiegate scandal were deemed qualified for their respective position, but many received premium posts that "ordinarily take career officers more than 20 years to attain." Wick also appointed more than 60 non-career officers to positions traditionally held by career personnel. Critics complained that the move, including other personnel shifts in the agency, severely damaged morale within the agency.

Wick and the Speaker Blacklist

In yet another investigation – this one conducted by USIA Office of Inspections – Wick was associated with a document which allegedly blacklisted a number of liberals who were suggested for overseas speaking assignments for the AmParts Program, USIA overseas speaker program which sends over 500 speakers each year to Europe, Asia, Africa, and Latin America.

The document contained handwritten notes and objections from current and former agency officials for 84 individuals under consideration as participants, and was circulated weekly among Wick's top deputies who selected the participants. The list included such names as Walter Cronkite, David Brinkley, John Kenneth Galbraith, Benjamin Bradlee, Tom Wicker, Betty Friedan, Coretta Scott King, Ralph Nader, Gary Hart, Arnaud de Borchgrave, and Douglas Feith.

In a letter to the Subcommittee on International Operations, Tom Harvey, USIA General Counsel explained that the blacklist was not known by Wick (there was no evidence that Wick knew about the blacklisting) and had he been aware of it, he (Wick) would not have sanctioned it. Harvey also admitted destroying all copies of the blacklist after discussing such action with Joe Boerner, the Senior Inspector on the AmParts Inspection project.

USIA Inspector General's Office launched another investigation on Wick for his use of the diplomatic pouch for a letter he sent to Alexander Kamshalov, chairman of the Soviet film distribution agency, Goskino. Wick had asked a USIA aide if the letter could be sent via pouch "but only if it were appropriate." Concerned about the appropriateness of sending the letter in this manner, he inquired whether or not it was acceptable and got an affirmative answer from a USIA aide. A USIA official at the U.S. embassy intercepted the letter and reported it as a possible breach of diplomatic privilege (Goshko, 1980).

While he received more public criticism than any other Reagan appointee, was perpetually enmeshed in controversy, had a poor public image, and had questionable management practices, the nation's chief publicist still managed to upgrade the image of USIA. He increased the agency's visibility and funding, modernized its technology, and transformed it into a major public diplomacy catalyst that improved East-West relations ("Wick legacy," 1988).

Though being at the center of conflict almost from the day that he became director of USIA, and despite his recurrent indiscretions, the consensus was that America's global information campaign had been strengthened rather than weakened under Charlie Wick's leadership. The agency, with greatly increased funding and representation in the inner circle of Washington's policy makers, had been transformed from a "government backwater into a key weapon in the battle of information and ideas that the Reagan administration waged with Russia" ("USIA, A," 1984, p. 58).

Wick and Anti-Communism

When Wick took over as director of USIA, he was seen as having "one of the most strident anti-Communist views in Washington" and was one of the most vocal anti-Communist voices in the Reagan administration. Trumpeting Reagan's hardline foreign policies, Wick was credited with making the agency an international propaganda arm and a partisan ideological weapon of the Reagan administration instead of a neutral purveyor of information (Howell, 1983; Madison, 1984).

To the degree it was known, Wick's ideology was hard right and anti-Communist. Wick was firmly in tune with the Reagan Administration's tendency to view the world more in East-West terms (Madison, 1984). Describing the Soviets disinformation efforts as mastery and providing numerous details about Soviet campaigns, he said the Russians were successful in planting false stories in "unwitting media" and were very successful in exploiting the "genuine, understandable concern" of individual citizens (Roderick, 1982).

In the early years of Wick's directorship, there was some concern that USIA focused predominantly on Soviet-oriented propaganda and had become the epicenter of U.S. efforts to counter Soviet propaganda ("USIA, A, 1988). Critics also accused him of attempting to politicize the agency with his "Reaganesque anti-communism" ("USIA: All," 1985).

Additionally, many of Wick critics believed that his alleged anti-Communist views would affect his ability to run USIA. Green described the tenor of the Wick-Reagan years like this:

...we, the good democracies...and they, the evil empire of the U.S.S.R. USIA would now fully reflect this outlook. No longer would the U.S. stand mute in the face of Communist vilification. No longer would the nation compete shyly in the idea marts of the world. It was time, in the Wick-Reagan partnership, for America to speak up (Green, 1988, p. 93).

In early speeches he gave throughout the U.S., Wick explained to audiences that the Soviet Union was spending many times more than the United States both in money and personnel to influence the young people of the world. Facts Wick often used repeatedly about the Soviet Union included: 1) the Soviet Union was outspending the U.S by six to one in public diplomacy; 2) their efforts were evidence of disinformation or misinformation; 3) they spent more money jamming VOA in Eastern Europe than VOA's entire budget; and 4) they have 70,000 employees; VOA has 7,500.

His orations also included descriptions of how USIA had launched several projects to counter Soviet disinformation. Initiated in 1981 were:

- *Fast Guidance Service* – cables USIA sent to embassies which detailed specific information used to rebut Soviet disinformation
- *Dateline America* – articles highlighting American strengths, achievements, and ideals for placement in magazines and newspapers throughout the world

- *Soviet Military Power* – a booklet by USIA describing the Soviet capability
- A pamphlet on Afghanistan, describing the Soviet Union's occupation of the nation.

The list also included *Soviet Propaganda Alert,* a publication that exposed Soviet disinformation around the world. The original report series was called Soviet Propaganda Alert, Project Truth. The secondary heading Project Truth was later dropped. The title Soviet Propaganda Alert was subsequently changed to Soviet Propaganda Trends. A former author noted that the monthly publication summarized Soviet statements about arms control, foreign relations, regional issues, bilateral relations, and human rights. The publication never included the author's name (Righetti, 1993).

Correspondingly, during a House appropriations subcommittee meeting, Wick requested approval of a $1 billion agency budget to combat "one of the most sophisticated and determined misinformation and disinformation efforts by the Soviet Union to influence public opinion." Wick's Soviet counterparts, including Radio Moscow, Tass, and Pravda, responded to his Soviet-bashing by describing him as a "master propagandist, a throwback to Joseph Goebbels."

It was also reported that the Kremlin detested him, and in a 1984 radio broadcast, the announcer dubbed him the "Goebbels of America" and called his plans for beaming U.S. government-made TV shows to Russia "television propagandist aggression."

Early in his tenure as USIA director, Wick made attempts with Soviet leaders to establish constructive dialogues to further mutual understanding. Over the years, his anti-Soviet attitude softened, and his attempts to counter Soviet campaigns of disinformation with USIA media tools were replaced with conciliatory attempts to facilitate East-West cooperation (Weinraub, 1986).

Wick was also the first USIA director to visit the Soviet Union, visiting the country four times. After those visits, he sought exchanges of people, books, movies, and VOA broadcasts. In 1986, he suggested that President Reagan and General Secretary Gorbachev address each other's people on New Year's Day.

Wick has also been credited with facilitating a secret disinformation pact with the Soviets. Wick met with Leonid Kravchenko, director of the Soviet news agency TASS to discuss disinformation detente and to seek permission to broadcast VOA programming on domestic radio stations in the Soviet Union in return for allowing Moscow stations to broadcast on U.S. radio stations. Anderson & Van Atta (1989) explained the details of the meeting:

> The talks began because Wick got fed up with the lies and Soviet jamming of Voice of America radio broadcasts. He asked the Soviets to ease up...In January 1987, on a trip to Moscow when the Soviets were signing the medium range missile treaty, Wick asked Soviet officials how they could expect to be trusted "if you keep putting out a lot of lies about us." That bluntness got Wick invited to lunch with Mikhail Gorbachev when the Soviet leader came to Washington in December 1987. Wick told Gorbachev that if he were "really serious about reducing tension and strain," he would stop lies and the jamming of Voice of America.

Wick returned from the Soviet Union with an "uncharacteristic optimism" about future U.S.-Soviet relations. Wick's conciliatory efforts continued after his subsequent visits to the Soviet Union. He orchestrated the historic information talks held in Washington in April of 1988 and invited sixteen high level Soviet information and media officials to meet at USIA headquarters with agency officials, media representatives and several communication institutions to discuss information exchanges between the two countries.

Wick conceded that there had been a pendulum swing in his ideological leanings and with that change came increased attempts to forge a new and more open relationship with the Soviets. He stressed that despite his views about Communism, his mission all along was to present America's story to the world.

Wick maintained that he was supporting Reagan's goal to present America's story to the world and not merely espousing his own ideologies. He suggested that he did not join USIA as the "chief apostle of a right-wing take-over and the chief subverting agent of a conspiracy to bend USIA and the Voice of America to our philosophy." There may be people who wanted to do that, he said, but Congress made it very clear that that was against the rules.

Wick often confirmed the fact that Reagan's ideology – being "deadly serious about his mission to demolish the image that the Soviets seek (sic) to paint the United States as a warmonger" – was his ideology. He supported President Reagan beliefs that information was a strategic component of national security, the infrastructure of democracy must be fostered overseas, there must be a peaceful competition of ideas and values with the Soviets, and public diplomacy was important to the United States. He passionately explained in a personal interview:

It wasn't Charlie Wick's ideology that was being promoted. When we blanketed the world with the various resources of USIA, it was with policies of the Reagan administration. We were advancing the policies of the U.S. government. I believe that I was conscientious and resourceful in representing America and not just one man's ideology (Wick, 1992).

Wick's life, as chronicled in his words, was one long propaganda war. He appeared to be engaged in an eternal battle to defend his personal image and that of USIA, the Reagan administration, and U.S. foreign policy, more or less in that order (Kurtz, 1985).

A survivor of numerous scrapes, Wick completed many of the important tasks he set out to accomplish during his eight-year term as USIA Director. He assisted with the increased funding for the agency and obtained an expanding budget during times when other agencies experienced tightened spending.

Thirty-six months after Charles Wick became President Ronald Reagan's USIA Director, the agency budget grew 42 percent, one of the largest hikes in agency funding during the Reagan era. He infused the agency with energy; directed the inauguration of Worldnet; expanded cultural programs and doubled Fulbright exchanges; implemented an exchange agreement between President Reagan and General Secretary Gorbachev in Geneva; created Radio Marti; and led discussions with the Soviets on media reciprocity, jamming, disinformation, and free flow issues ("Summary," 1988).

Wick and Worldnet

Wick had a tendency to treat Worldnet as an only child in an agency with far too many orphans. Calling Worldnet his television equivalent of Voice of America, he credited the service with billions of viewer impressions and was very methodical in generating a cadre of people in defense of the service.

After an interactive program, posts were required to report the media reactions and the audience numbers for that particular program. Details of those cables, including comments and audience numbers, were compiled and analyzed, then used in an extensive letter campaign on Capitol Hill. Key guests of the interactives received glowing highlights about their particular interactive. Those guests would then quote the numbers on other occasions, or would use the numbers they received from USIA in letters or memos to Congress when supporting Wick or the Worldnet service.

Then, Worldnet officials used key guests' comments – especially those received in response to the original letters sent by USIA – in their news releases, reports to Congress, and to embassies via cable.

USIA, in a sense, created its own public relations response mechanism that was able to route the favorable information full circle. In summaries vital to the justification of the program, one could find numerous comments (favorable, of course) from the network's guests.

Part of the program's success was rationalized by the positive response from those key guests – the participants in the interactives, explained Galbraith:

The other wonderful thing about Worldnet is whenever the committee would make a criticism; a member would quickly come up and say, "What? You don't know what you are talking about. I just got a letter from Weinberger last week, and he said it was great. Let me send you a copy of the letter. It's an interesting idea that you're gonna measure

the success of television programs by the reaction of those who are on
television rather than those who are viewing it (Galbraith, 1990).

Wick's Friendship with the President

Some surmise USIA's profile was elevated to its highest point
because of Wick's friendship with President Reagan. A friend
since their Hollywood days, President Reagan supported Wick
and his activities within USIA, including the inauguration of
Worldnet and the increased funding for the agency.

The friendship began in the 1960s when the children of both
families attended the same private school in Bel Air, California.
The wives of Wick and Reagan carpooled each other's children
and worked together on various charities. Mary Jane Wick was
considered to be one of Nancy Reagan's closest friends.

Nineteen years into the friendship, Wick and his wife decided
to assist Reagan with his fund-raising activities for the presidential
race. Wick explained their participation in Reagan fund-raising
efforts:

> *We decided to have a luncheon for Ronnie and invite some heavy*
> *hitters to come and meet him. We fashioned a mailgram asking*
> *people to join us for the first meeting of the "Ground Floor*
> *Committee." The mailgram said, "Please join us in the formation of*
> *the Ground Floor Committee at our house June 28, 1979. P.S. The next*
> *meeting will be at the White House." To ensure the success of the*
> *gathering and not have to worry about the tragedy of having no-*
> *shows, we asked 10 or 11 people to be co-signatories at a cost of $1,000*
> *per person. We all felt confident the event would be a success. It was.*
> *Our first gathering raised $80,000 (Wick, 1992).*

After the $1,000-a-guest cocktail party, the Wicks formed the Reagan $10,000 club and put together an impressive list of 350 people who pledged to raise the funds. In August 1979, Wick met with Reagan and suggested to him that he begin his campaign in New York City with the official announcement of his intention to run for the presidency. Wick intended to set up another successful Ground Floor Committee there. Utilizing his seemingly tireless fund-raising efforts and well-honed public relations and entrepreneurial skills, Wick spent two more years raising over $10 million for Reagan's campaign.

Once the nomination was finalized, the Republican National Committee selected Wick and his wife to direct the "Prelude to Victory" Dinners for Reagan that netted another $5 million. With co-chair Robert Gray, vice-president of Hill & Knowlton, the world's largest public relations firm, Wick masterminded Reagan's eight-million-dollar inauguration, the most expensive in American history.

Early in his presidential campaign, Ronald Reagan noted that a "stronger information effort would be part of his plan to make the United States more respected in the world." Wick was appointed USIA Director to carry out Reagan's edict.

While it was well known that Wick was a personal friend of President Ronald Reagan and a member of the President's so-called kitchen cabinet, Wick pointed out that his friendship with the President was never exploited:

My friendship with the President helped enormously...but I never exploited the power that was given to me. I was not interested in self-aggrandizement (Wick, 1990).

According to McBride, there didn't seem to be any favors thrown Wick's way just because he was a friend of President Reagan. The public diplomacy function of the U.S. government had long been neglected, and it happened that Wick was director of USIA when awareness increased and funding was made available. This, coupled with Wick's aggressiveness for the cause of harnessing modem technology to revolutionize the field of public diplomacy and his apparent instinct for innovation, created an environment ripe for the birth of an international government-sponsored television service.

Additionally, both Reagan and Wick were media moguls – masters of public relations who understood the art of communication and publicity. These men were able to stimulate interest for their causes.

Hollywood Hype and State-of-the-Art Technology

In the end, any assessment of Charles Wick's stewardship as director of the U.S. Information Agency did not hinge on whether he was universally beloved at the agency or Capitol Hill, or if he knew anything about assessing audiences, but on whether or not he enhanced or undermined the agency's credibility.

Through his personality and management style, and possibly even his friendship with the President, Wick amassed a list of accomplishments no USIA director before him could approach. He is credited with bringing USIA into the forefront of international communication "with a mix of Hollywood hype and state-of-the-art satellite technology" to fulfill the agency's mission.

Wick energized and strengthened the agency responsible for America's public diplomacy efforts abroad and finally earned applause from his critics who saw him transform a run-down agency into one of the most prosperous in the Reagan administration.

In the end, even after Wick's management of the agency had been scrutinized by the Congress, the press, the GAO, USIA's own inspectors, and specialists on public diplomacy, the director remained a contradictory puzzle, even to some of those who had worked most closely with him. He was an illustration of contrasts: a man who had tremendous energy and intelligence and a man with revealing and notorious gaffes.

CHAPTER SEVEN

Restrictions on Worldnet

The 1990 Foreign Relations authorization bill reauthorized a restricted Worldnet service and prescribed details on how its direction should be shaped. Worldnet received the permission to reinstate passive programming, but network executives were restricted to buying programs from private sources rather than producing the programs themselves. Galbraith (1990) had his own interpretation of the restrictions.

They are not going to have their own network. Instead they are going to use satellite technology as a means to deliver television products to other countries...for rebroadcast...that can be used for viewing in other countries. If you look at television in the Third World, or Pakistan, they are begging for products...So, in that sense, if a satellite can deliver high quality products like National Geographic, they are going to use it. That's what the new USIA program will do. It's not going to be an American state program, or a USIA news program. Nobody would use it; nobody would watch it. This is a modest approach – consistent with the amount of money we have at this time (Galbraith, 1990).

Bruce suggested that besides dealing with reduced funding, one of the network's major hurdles was to establish credibility in the traditional sense – that statements made about the network and its audience needed to be credible.

My concern is that they will go back to the heyday, being like wild cowboys...just doing everything in sight with no particular organization, no logic...that's my greatest concern (Bruce, 1990).

While Worldnet was one of America's most innovative public diplomacy programs, the experimental service was caught in the middle of a common bureaucratic turf war. Wick's directorship laid the groundwork for a tightened Congressional reign regarding unsupervised spending and the operation of a service that had followed no set guidelines or restrictions. Congress prevented Worldnet from proceeding in the "wild cowboy" fashion Bruce described.

From 1983 to 1989, Wick was the driving force behind Worldnet and satellite television in the service of U.S. public diplomacy. Worldnet was not the number one priority of the director before Wick, nor was it high on the priority list of 1990 USIA Director Bruce Gelb, former New York pharmaceutical executive and President George Bush's replacement for Charles Wick.

Gelb was determined not to repeat Worldnet's past problems, and was committed to not repeating the problems experienced by Wick and work closely with Congress to ensure that USIA's use of satellite communication was prudent and cost effective.

In the end, Worldnet was a strategic and tactical resource in those instances it responded to world events defending and explaining the U.S. policy stance not only in the case of Grenada, Libya, but in numerous other instances.

Diplomats communicated the substance of U.S. policies to other governments during the interactives. Besides those interviews, Worldnet did little to establish itself as a strident policy mechanism.

Furthermore, little evidence was available to suggest that Worldnet staff had direct access to information necessary to create a "policy advocacy" stance. In general, government officials transmit government policy. Other programming material rarely contained U.S. policy directives.

In March 1986, only two weeks prior to the Libyan strike, President Reagan called for a worldwide ban on chemical weapons. Within 12 hours of that ban, then Vice-President George Bush was discussing the proposal with key journalists in seven European countries.

Thirteen hours after the U.S. air strike against Libya in April 1986, Worldnet staff directed three successive interactives in London, Paris, Bonn, Rome, and Madrid to explain U.S. policy on the action. Secretary of State, George Shultz and Secretary of Defense, Caspar Weinberger spoke directly with journalists in Europe and in Latin America.

Time and again, USIA staff demonstrated the ability to respond quickly with authoritative policy explication to key audiences via Worldnet. During the 1991 Desert Storm activity in the Middle East, Worldnet supported every major U.S. move with broadcasts to the region informing foreign citizens about U.S. foreign policy.

The concentrated effort included combatting disinformation about U.S. bombing activities, and supplying additional details on major U.S. diplomatic moves, and military actions (Hinker, 1992).

⌘

In March 1992, USIA has 280 TVROs. Every embassy and consulate around the world was equipped with a satellite dish to receive Worldnet's interactive and passive programming. By early 1992, Worldnet had aired over 2,5000 interactives.

CHAPTER EIGHT

Was Worldnet Propaganda?

nalyses of propaganda activities require a working definition of the word. Despite the obvious problem of definition choice and interpretation of the various definitions available, there is a profound uncertainty among specialists about a precise definition for propaganda and what exactly can be labeled as propaganda.

Convinced that America's concept of propaganda should be broadened to include many forms of international communication, Davies (1966) espoused a broad definition of propaganda that encompassed a panoply of materials and activities. His definition, which was applicable for Worldnet, included "cultural relations, relations between education institutions, relations between scientists and technicians, relations between institutions and persons in the field of the creative and performing arts, and a whole panorama of activities..."

For Davies, propaganda was neutral and connoted merely a spreading of information.

Similarly broad, Lee's (1952) definition was simplistic at best, but adequately described Worldnet — "a way of conveying ideas rapidly to many people."

So, if a broad definition of propaganda is used — one that incorporates all types of communication activities — then, Worldnet can easily be labeled as propaganda. On the other hand, if a narrow or more specific definition is used, Worldnet as a propaganda medium can easily be eliminated from the framework. Worldnet operations do not fit the major constructs of Herman and Chomsky's (1988) narrowly defined, though important, contemporary model of propaganda for the following reasons: there was no profit orientation of the organization; advertising was not the principal income source; and anti-Communism was not used as a control mechanism. Cross-ownership and control by non-media companies was not possible with this type of government-owned, government-financed operation. This model has certain plausibility for the American media, but fails to address the nuances of Worldnet, a unique international government-owned and run media service.

Lasswell, Lemer, and Spier's (1979) definition helps to delineate between what is propaganda and what is information. Worldnet offers both. At times, the service offered programming which incorporated a "deliberate effort to influence the outcomes of controversy in favor of a preference," while at other times it merely transmitted information. The service made deliberate attempts to spread information in the international environment. The approach was planned, and the public communication was directed towards a mass audience whose minds may or may not have been affected. Worldnet attempted to invade with its ideas of America, and sought to influence, direct and strengthen attitudes along some pre-determined lines.

As an ideological instrument, it did attempt to "induce or stimulate politically significant attitudes and behaviors" favorable to America and to the U.S. Government (O'Brien, 1966). Whether or not Worldnet psychologically unified a mass of individuals through its methods was hard to assess.

Unlike Stalinist propaganda that was founded on Pavlov's theory of conditioned reflex, and Hitlerian propaganda on Freud's theory of repression and libido, American propaganda, including the propaganda from Worldnet, is based on John Dewey's theory of teaching. The information offered by the service appeared to be rational and factual.

Two significant models employed in this analysis, are Ellul's sociological model and his political propaganda model. Both of these models follow the requirements of what Ellul described as horizontal propaganda – that which involves a huge organization of people, propaganda made inside the group, and all individuals being equal.

Both offer numerous applicable precepts for analyzing the form and function of a propaganda medium. While each model has numerous dimensions, not all of the conditions of each apply to Worldnet. Worldnet was both sociological and political propaganda. However, it met more of the conditions of the sociological model.

Worldnet used numerous social currents, acted in a "gentle" manner, and was aimed at long-term penetration and adaptation of ideas. The network, in fact, constituted an ideal framework for sociological propaganda, though its efforts were somewhat diffuse.

In the network's promulgation of ideas and prejudices, it championed a style of life rather than a specific doctrine or formal adherence to that doctrine.

Worldnet offered political propaganda, in that, its programs had themes and objectives that were political, had political ends, and involved techniques of influence employed by a government to change behavior. Additionally, the network sometimes exhibited an approach that sought immediate results.

Worldnet offerings could be labeled propaganda, but the service was no highly developed propaganda system. Notably from Ellul's expanded model of propaganda, Worldnet staff were not "properly-trained propagandists" who were using, with an exacting precision, advanced sociological and psychological principles, nor was there evidence that they applied precise formulas of psychological warfare. They were not a group of what Ellul called "technicians of influence." Additionally, there was scant evidence to suggest that Worldnet or its program offerings were "conceived in the secret recesses of political enclaves."

Ellul's precision in describing the nature of propaganda and his all-inclusive models of propaganda are limiting to this analysis. For Ellul, many things can be propaganda, but interestingly, one specific communication medium would not be able to meet all of the poignant requirements and prescriptions to which he ascribes.

Ellul also posits descriptions of propaganda in terms of "the enemy." Though his models are applicable for analyzing Worldnet during the time period when both agency officials and the Reagan Administration had anti-Soviet stances, the models, utility and applicability lessen as the anti-Soviet attitudes waned. Essentially, using propaganda analysis couched only in "war terms" is limiting for the analysis of a peacetime operation.

Worldnet was not a dictatorial, propaganda device, but a device of peacetime. The Worldnet service offerings were a type of propaganda that contributed to world peace, and ultimately, supported the peaceful relations between countries, while still supporting U.S. foreign policy objectives.

Worldnet's programming was not disseminated for the purpose of upsetting the structure of international society. The primary focus was on mutual interest and understanding. The programming did not inspire confrontational behavior.

As peacetime propaganda, Worldnet's program offerings were not broadcast to intervene in the affairs of other nations or to negatively affect domestic regimes' ability to exercise governmental control. The network appeared to uphold the "legitimacy of the constituted government(s)" of foreign nations (Falk, 1966).

Worldnet, USIS, and USIA staffs were all cognizant of the technological and social differences that exist between countries, and were aware of the importance of sharing ideas despite these differences. Though programming dealt with both controversial and non-controversial issues, and possibly even changed attitudes, its primary focus seemed to be on socially beneficial ends. USIS officers suggested topics for Worldnet interactives, for example, which supported their respective country plans and which were of interest to individuals in that country.

Finally, Worldnet can be described as facilitative communication, international communication, political communication, public diplomacy, and other equally descriptive labels. As shown in this analysis, it is also propaganda, albeit a weak version.

In the end, all that matters is what one means by each of these terms. Semantic obstacles and attitudes towards different terms or labels that were used to describe elements of the U.S. Government information efforts overseas should not preclude the understanding that Worldnet was many things.

The propaganda disseminated by Worldnet had a sociological bent; however, the program's purpose was more to educate than to persuade or propagandize. Did Worldnet deliver propaganda? To those in democratic regimes that feel revulsion against the word propaganda, the answer would be no. To others, the label fit. In America, it was "safe" to say that Worldnet was a tool of public diplomacy. For those in the U.S. who wanted to kill Worldnet, it was propaganda.

With any scientific explanation that incorporates objective analysis, precision is affected by erroneous assumptions—in this case, of what is seen as bad (propaganda), and of what is seen as good (public diplomacy). When you analyze Worldnet's offerings – the output of the network – it must be done without an analysis of the intent of Worldnet's operators. Interpretation of intentions and intended meanings of messages is also difficult task. One is safe in analyzing only output.

Similarly, people differ on their definition of reality, their interpretation of human events, and in a fundamental way, differ in their approach for the quest of truth. In any analysis, one must not automatically conclude that propaganda is all lies or that truthfulness is what it appears to be.

The service, which was both vexatious and interesting, was created during an era when major changes were occurring between the former Soviet Union and the United States, and there was the dissolution of bipolar domination. At this time, the nature of contemporary global politics required a different approach to communication. And, though Worldnet's approach, or orchestration, was somewhat different from other international television services, it was far from being a soloist in its attempts to reach a foreign audience.

An international, peacetime, information operation with an interactive element, Worldnet was established to sell America's story abroad. As already noted, it was called many things: a tool of public diplomacy, mere propaganda, a "Machiavellian, beady-eyed approach" to information dissemination, an education and information purveyor, and much more.

While models of propaganda may be outdated for analysis of peacetime operations, so are the negative attitudes towards the term and the association of propaganda with Goebbels and wartime activities. However, the label will likely never shed its baggage.

Perhaps propaganda deserves a new definition. But, if we believe what Ellul says about propaganda – that everything is propaganda – then, even that (a new definition) is not necessary.

Ascribing the label "propaganda" to the Worldnet service was easy and convenient, but not fully appropriate. In Worldnet's case, propaganda (like beauty) was in the eyes of the beholder.

⌘

People all over the world desire a global order based on humane values and humane government responses to needs and aspirations. Government-to-people communication must always be a part of government efforts for diplomacy. Information should be freely available and not be severed from diplomatic or economic strategies. Information can provide an eloquent testimony for the freeing of the human spirit and for stimulating the self-determination of the people.

Worldnet had an important purpose in the public diplomacy efforts and history of the United States. It was positioned to use information for facilitating human betterment and pursuing peaceful coexistence. If the U.S. government, through Worldnet, provided information that helped others to identify and address the need to be free and stimulated a quest for world peace, then its efforts were not wasted. What people called Worldnet is inconsequential.

CHAPTER NINE

Selected Bibliography

Abshire, D. (1976). **International broadcasting: A new dimension in western diplomacy**. Georgetown Center for Strategic and International Studies (CSIS), Washington Papers, 35. Beverly Hills, CA: Sage.

Alexandre, L. (1988). **The Voice of America: From detente to the Reagan Doctrine.** Norwood, NJ: Ablex Publishing Corporation.

Anderson, J. & Van Atta, D. (1989, October 24). Soviets back off disinformation drive. **Washington Post**, D34.

Anderson, J. & Van Atta, D. (1989b, November 3). Loaded for bear. **Washington Post**, E5.

A study of USIA operating assumptions. (1954). Washington,

DC: United States Information Agency.

Bailey, G. (1984). **Armageddon in prime time.** New York: Avon.

Bailey, T. (1946). **A diplomatic history of the American people.** New York, NY: F.S. Crofts & Co.

Barghoom, F. (1950). **The Soviet image of the United States.** New York: Harcourt, Brace & Co.

Bartlett, F. (1940). **Political propaganda.** Cambridge: Cambridge University Press.

BBC to test feasibility of world satellite. (1985). Variety, 135.

Beard, J. (1992, March). [**Personal Interview**]. Congressional Liaison Officer, United States Information Agency. Washington, DC.

Bell, B. (1989). **USIA/TV and the future use of satellite television.** United States Information Agency (Draft Document).

Bernays, E. & Hershey, B. (Eds.). (1970). **The case for reappraisal of U.S. overseas information programs.** (Special Studies in International Politics and Special Affairs). New York: Praeger Publishers.

Binder, D. (1988, June 2). Wick finds a high profile need not be a target. **New York Times,** 137, B10.

Blume, W. (1977). In United States House of Representatives. Subcommittee on International Operations, Committee on International Operations. Hearings. **Public diplomacy and the future.** (June 8-24). Washington, DC: United States Government Printing Office.

Boyd, D. (1985). A study of future directions for the Voice of America in the changing world of international broadcasting. Journal of Broadcasting and Electronic Media, 29, 215-217.

Bremer, J. (1986, April). [Unclassified Telegram from the Hague to the United States Information Agency]. Washington, DC.

Bruce, T. (1990, January). [Personal interview]. Staff Consultant, House Foreign Affairs Committee. Washington, DC.

Bruntz, G. (1938). Allied propaganda and the collapse of the German empire in 1918. London: Humphrey Milford.

Bruun, G. & Lee, D. (1964). The second World War and after. Boston: Houghton Mifflin Company.

Buchanan, J. (1977). In United States House of Representatives. Subcommittee on International Operations, Committee on International Operations. Hearings. Public diplomacy and the future. (June 8-24). Washington, DC: United States Government Printing Office.

Buitenhuis, P. (1987). The great war of words: British American, and Canadian propaganda and fiction, 1914, 1933. Vancouver: University of British Columbia Press.

Bumpus, B. & Skelt, B. (1985). Seventy years of international broadcasting. Communication and Society, No. 14. Paris: UNESCO.

Burnett, S. (1985, September 19). Informing the foreign public. [Letter]. Christian Science Monitor, 77, 17.

Burnett, S. (1986). U.S. information and cultural programs. In R. Staar (Ed.), **Public diplomacy: USA versus USSR.** Stanford: Hoover Institution.

Burt, R. (1984, February 22). [**Letter to Charles Z. Wick**]. United States Department of State, Assistant Secretary of State for European Affairs. Washington, DC.

Campbell, S. (1987). **A map of the field: A summary and analysis of a questionnaire on public diplomacy.** The Kettering Foundation.

Can the news abroad come home? The United States Information Agency. (1987, Nov. 24). **New York Times, 137,** B8.

Carter, A. (1970). The state of the art: Communications and foreign affairs. **Foreign Service Journal,** 47, 31-21, 46-47.

Casting the net. (1988). **Euroview,** 34, 7-8.

Castle, E. (1955). **Billions, blunders, and baloney: The fantastic story of how Uncle Sam is squandering your money overseas.** New York, NY: Devin-Adair Co., Inc.

Christopher, W. (1977). In United States House of Representatives. Subcommittee on International Operations, Committee on International Operations. Hearings. **Public diplomacy and the future.** (June 8-24). Washington, DC: United States Government Printing Office.

Comptroller General. United States General Accounting Office. (1977, December 10). **Public diplomacy in the years ahead – An assessment of proposals for reorganization. Report to**

Congress. Washington, DC: United States Government Printing Office.

Comptroller General. United States General Accounting Office. (1979). **The public diplomacy of other countries: Implications for the United States.** Report to Congress. Washington, DC: United States Government Printing Office.

Courter, J. (1987). **Public diplomacy in the information age.** Washington, DC: United States Advisory Commission on Public Diplomacy Conference.

Crossman, R. (1952). Psychological warfare. **The Journal of the Royal United Service Institution, 97,** 319-332.

Daugherty, W. (Ed.). (1958). **A psychological warfare casebook.** Baltimore: John Hopkins University Press.

David, M. & Aufderheide, P. (1985). All the president's media. **Channels of Communication, 5,** 20-24.

Davidson, P. (1987). **Wick announces Worldnet news charter: Patterned on VOA document.** USIA News Release. Washington, DC: United States Information Agency.

Davie, M. (1985, July 7). Uncle Sam gets message across on celestial TV. **The Observer, 44.**

Davies, R. (1966). The American commitment to public propaganda. **Law and Contemporary Problems, 31,** 452-458.

Davis, J. (1984, January/February). Thousands of miles of cable and hundreds of technicians. **USIA World, 7,** 14.

Deibel, T. & Roberts, W. (1976). **Culture and information:**

Two foreign policy functions. Georgetown Center for Strategic and International Studies Washington Papers (CSIS), 40. Beverly Hills, CA: Sage.

Demitz, S. (1990, January). [Personal interview]. Chief, Office of Media Research. Office of Research. United States Information Agency. Washington, DC.

Dizard, W. (1961). The strategy of truth. Washington, DC: Public Affairs Press.

Dougan, D. (1985). The challenges of the new information age: Agenda for a new bureau. Foreign Service Institute Symposium on International Communications, Technology, and Foreign Policy. Washington, DC.

Eames, B. (1990, January). [Personal interview]. Assistant Director, Worldnet, United States Information Agency. Washington, DC.

Effron, E. (1984). USIA boss, phone tapes raise moral and legal issues: Pressure to resign. Los Angeles Daily Journal, 97, 1.

Electronic liberation. (1984, February 1). Oklahoma Daily Press, 2.

Ellul, J. (1965). Propaganda: The formation of men's attitudes. New York: Alfred A. Knopf.

Fact sheet. Television and Film Service. (1989). Washington, DC: United States Information Agency.

Falk, R. (1966). On regulating international propaganda: A plea for moderate aims. Law and Contemporary Problems, 31, 601-621.

Farnsworth, S. (1984). Worldnet television system viewed as valuable tool in explaining America's position during times of crisis. **Los Angeles Times**, 2, I-A.

Fascell, D. (1977). In United States House of Representatives. Subcommittee on International Operations, Committee on International Operations. Hearings. **Public diplomacy and the future.** (June 8-24). Washington, DC: United States Government Printing Office.

Fascell, D. (1985). **International communications policy: Preparing for the future.** The Third David M. Abshire Endowed Lecture, October 5. Center for Strategic and International Studies Significant Issues Series, 3. Washington, DC: Center for Strategic and International Studies (CSIS).

Fascell, D. (1986). In United States House of Representatives. Subcommittee on International Operations, Committee on International Operations. Hearings. **Oversight of Public Diplomacy.** 99th Congress. (July 16, 23; August 6; & September 6).

Feulner, E. (1986). In United States House of Representatives. Subcommittee on International Operations, Committee on International Operations. Hearings. Oversight of Public Diplomacy. 99th Congress. (July 16, 23; August 6; & September 6).

Fields, H. (1985). U.S. overseas broadcast service expanding. **Television-Radio Age, 33,** 38-39.

Fisher, G. (1972). **Public diplomacy and the behavioral sciences.**

Bloomington: Indiana University Press.

Fitchett, J. (1985). U.S. to use new satellite television link abroad. **International Herald Tribune, 4.**

Fouquet, D. (1985, May 16). U.S. uses new 'weapon' in war of ideas with USSR. **Christian Science Monitor,** 77, 32.

Galbraith, P. (1990). [**Personal Interview**]. Senior Staff Member, Senate Foreign Relations Committee. Washington, DC.

Gallup, G. (1977). In United States House of Representatives. Subcommittee on International Operations, Committee on International Operations. Hearings. **Public diplomacy and the future.** (June 8-24).

Gelb, B. (1989). [**Letter to The Honorable Lawrence Smith, Foreign Affairs Committee**]. USIA Historical Collection. Washington, DC: United States Information Agency.

German equivalent of Worldnet? Unclassified document. [**Incoming Telegram to USIA**]. (1985, May). American Embassy, Bonn, Germany.

Godson, D. (1987). **SDI: Has America told her story to the world?** Washington, DC: Institute for Foreign Policy Analysis, Inc.

Goodfriend, A. (1963). **The twisted image.** New York: St. Martin's Press.

Goodpaster, A. & Seignious, G. II. (1987). **United States international leadership for the 21st century: Building a national foreign affairs constituency.** Joint Working Group of the Atlantic Council of the United States and the Citizens Network for Foreign Affairs.

Gordon, G. & Falk, I. (1973). **The war of ideas.** New York, NY: Hastings House Publisher.

Gordon, G., Falk, I., & Hodap, W. (1963). **The idea invaders.** New York, NY: Hastings House.

Goshko, J. (1986, March 31). Talk not cheap at Wick's USIA: Well-funded propaganda machine pursues 'public diplomacy.' **Washington Post, 109,** Al.

Grantham, B. (1986, March 12). Sky Channel's hefty schedule of U.S. programs plays better in north than southern Europe. **Variety,** 27.

Green, F. (1988). **American propaganda abroad.** New York: Hippocrene Books.

Greene, J. (1951). **A study of communist propaganda and agitation directed against the armed forces of the United States.** (Dissertation). Washington, DC: Georgetown University.

Gregory, B. (1990, January). [**Personal interview**]. Staff Director, United States Advisory Commission on Public Diplomacy. Washington, DC.

Gregory, B. (1987). **Charter of the United States Advisory Commission on Public Diplomacy.** Washington, DC: United States Information Agency.

Halliday, F. (1983). **The making of the second cold war.** London: Verson Editions.

Hansen, A. (1984). **USIA: Public diplomacy in the computer age** New York: Praeger Publishers.

Harvey, T. (1984). [**Letter to The Subcommittee on International Operations**]. USIA Historical Collection. Washington, DC: United States Information Agency.

Heflin, H. (1988, August 2). [**Letter to United States Senator Claiborne Pell, Chairman, Committee on Foreign Relations, United States Senate**]. Washington, DC.

Hemming, J. (1983, December). USIA's first Euronet telecast links Washington with five European Embassies. **USIA World**, 4-5, 16.

Henderson, G. (1973). **Public diplomacy and political change.** New York; Praeger Publishers.

Henderson, J. (1968). **The United States Information Agency.** New York, London, Washington; Praeger Publishers.

Herman, E. & Chomsky, N. (1988). **Manufacturing consent: The political economy of the mass media.** New York: Pantheon Books.

Hickey, N. (1987). Worldnet fires away in the 'Star Wars' of ideas. **TV Guide, 35,** 10-12.

Hill cautious on authorizing competition to Intelsat. (1985, February 25). **Broadcasting,** 61.

Hinker, E. (1992, March). [**Personal interview**]. United States Information Agency, Office of Public Liaison. Washington, DC.

Hitchcock, D., Jr. (1988). **U.S. public diplomacy.** Washington,

DC: Center for Strategic and International Studies (CSIS).

Holt, R. & van de Velde, R. (1960). **Strategic psychological operations and American foreign policy.** Chicago, IL: University of Chicago Press.

Hornik, R. (1974). **Mass media and the 'revolution of rising Frustrations': A reconsideration of theory.** Papers of the East West Communication Institute, 11.

Howell, L. (1983). Revamping the image of America: At the nation's PR agency, Reaganism reigns. **Christianity and Crisis, 43,** 407-409.

Howell, W. (1986). **World broadcasting in the age of the satellite.** Norwood, NJ: Ablex.

Hughes, J. (1988, August 8). Don't weaken USIA: War of words continues. **The Wall Street Journal,** 14.

Joseph, T. & Singh, I. (1989). Worldnet's funding dilemma. **Satellite Communications, 13,** pp-29-30.

Joyce, W. (1963). **The propaganda gap.** New York, NY: Harper & Row.

Kalb, B. (1986). In United States House of Representatives. Subcommittee on International Operations, Committee on International Operations. Hearings. **Oversight of Public Diplomacy.** 99th Congress. (July 16, 23; August 6; & September 6).

Kaplan, P. (1985, April 23). U.S. agency transmits TV programs to Europe. **New York Times, 131,** C18.

Katz, E. (1979). With what effect? The lessons from

international communications research. In R. Merton (Ed.), **Qualitative and quantitative social research.** New York: Free Press.

Keogh, J. (1977). In United States House of Representatives. Subcommittee on International Operations, Committee on International Operations. Hearings. **Public diplomacy and the future.** (June 8-24). Washington, DC: United States Government Printing Office.

Kirkpatrick, L. & Sergeant, H. (1972). **Soviet political warfare techniques: Espionage and propaganda in the 1970s.** New York: National Strategy Information Center.

Kline, R. (1988). **President to address Europe via Worldnet: Other top U.S. officials slated for pre-summit dialogues.** (News Release). Washington, DC: United States Information Agency.

Kline, R. (1988b). **Worldnet's cable audience up by over one million homes.** (News Release). Washington, DC: United States Information Agency.

Kline, R. (1988c). **Worldnet extends global reach into Pacific ocean region.** (News Release). Washington, DC: United States Information Agency.

Kris, E. & Leites, N. (1951). Trends in twentieth century propaganda. In D. Lemer (Ed.), Propaganda in war and crisis. New York: George W. Stewart, Publisher, Inc.

Kurtz, H. (1984, January 20). Satellite news conferences help U.S. spread its message. The Washington Post, A9.

Lackey, A. (1948). **The psychological aspects of revolutionary propaganda.** (Dissertation). Washington, DC: Georgetown University.

Lasswell, H. (1927). **Propaganda in the world war.** New York: Knopf.

Lasswell, H. (1946). Describing the effects of communicating. In B. Smith, H. Lasswell and R. Casey (Ed.), **Propaganda, communication, and public opinion.** Princeton: Princeton University Press.

Lasswell, H. & Blumenstock, D. (1939). **World revolutionary propaganda: A Chicago study.** Chicago, IL: The University of Chicago Press.

Lasswell, H., Casey, R., & Smith. B. (1969). **Propaganda and promotional activities.** Chicago and London: The University of Chicago Press.

Lasswell, H., Lemer, D., & Spier, H. (Eds.). (1980). **Propaganda and communication in world history. Vol. I: Emergence of public opinion in the west.** Honolulu: The University Press of Hawaii.

Laurin, R. (Ed.). (1982). **Military propaganda-psychological warfare and operations.** New York: Praeger.

Lavine, H. & Wechsler, J. (1940). **War propaganda and the United States.** New Haven: Yale University Press.

Lee, A. (1952). **How to understand propaganda.** New York: Rinehart & Company, Inc.

Legeron, D. (1985). U.S.: Worldnet starts a crusade. **Le Monde,** 9.

Lemer, D. (Ed.). (1951). **Propaganda in war crisis.** New York: George Stewart, Publisher, Inc.

Lewis, H. (1977). In United States House of Representatives. Subcommittee on International Operations, Committee on International Operations. Hearings. **Public diplomacy and the future.** (June 8-24). Washington, DC: United States Government Printing Office.

Lewis, N. (1985, June 26). Wick is surviving the criticism. **New York Times, 131,** A21.

Littlejohn, S. (1983). **Theories of human communication.** Belmont, CA: Wadsworth Publishing Company.

Madison, C. (1984). Under Wick, USIA has a bigger budget, new digs and an image problem. **National Journal, 16,** 34-38.

Management of Public Diplomacy Relative to National Security. (1983, January 14). **National Security Directive 77.** Washington, DC: The White House.

Malone, G. (1988). **Political advocacy and cultural communication: Organizing the nation's diplomacy.** Lanham, MD: University Press of America.

Marks, L. (1977). In United States House of Representatives. Subcommittee on International Operations, Committee on International Operations. Hearings. **Public diplomacy and the future.** (June 8-24). Washington, DC: United States Government Printing Office.

McBride, R. (1992, March). [**Personal interview**]. Washington, DC.

Mica, D. (1987). **Public diplomacy in the information age.** Washington, DC: United States Advisory Commission on Public Diplomacy Conference.

Middendorf, J. (1984). [**Letter to Charles Z. Wick**]. United States Department of State, United States Permanent Mission to the Organization of American States. Washington, DC.

Mock, J. & Larson, C. (1939). Words that won the war. Princeton, NJ: Princeton University Press.

Moffett, G. (1987, June 23). UISA chief Charles Wick optimistic about US-Soviet relations. **Christian Science Monitor, 79,** 6.

Molotsky, I. (1986a, January 24). Wick has met the enemy. **New York Times, 135,** A16.

Molotsky, I. (1986b, May 8). Chernobyl and the 'global village.' **New York Times, 135,** A22.

Money's tight for USIA. (1987, May 18). **Broadcasting, 112,** 16.

Mundt, K. (1947, Nov. 9). We are losing the war of words in Europe. **New York Times Magazine,** 11, 61-63.

Mungo, P. (1984). Uncle Sam eyeing global TV web: USIA introduces 'Worldnet.' **Variety,** 317, 1-2.

Naylor, T. (1991). **The cold war legacy.** Lexington, MA: Lexington Books.

News over the Atlantic. Editorial. (1983, December 27). **The Wall Street Journal,** 5.

O'Brien, W. (1966). International propaganda and minimum world public order. **Law and Contemporary Problems,** 31, 589-600.

O'Connell, J. (1988a). **Congressional restriction forces USIA to cancel worldwide debate broadcasts.** (News Release). Washington, DC: United States Information Agency.

O'Connell, J. (1988b). **Congress fails to remove Worldnet restrictions; Agency convenes task force to evaluate options.** (News Release). Washington, DC: United States Information Agency.

Odom, L. (1977). In United States House of Representatives. Subcommittee on International Operations, Committee on International Operations. Hearings. **Public diplomacy and the future.** (June 8-24). Washington, DC: United States Government Printing Office.

Oseth, J. (1988). Public diplomacy and U.S. foreign policy. In Joseph S. Gordon, **Psychological operations: The Soviet challenge.** London: Westview Press.

Osterlund, P. (1985, October 21). With Wick at the helm, U.S. information is reborn: Bigger budget reflects effort to counter Soviets. **Christian Science Monitor,** 77, 3.

Paddock, A. (1986). U.S. informational and cultural programs. In R. Staar, (Ed.), **Public diplomacy: USA versus USSR.** Stanford: Hoover Institution. Pagano, P. (1985, March 2). TV goes global on Worldnet. **Los Angeles Times,** 1.

Pagano, P. (1985b, March 5). Information agency's global TV keeps world in touch with itself. **Orlando Sentinel,** E-8.

Pell, C. (1987). **Public diplomacy in the information age.**

Washington, DC: United States Advisory Commission on Public Diplomacy Conference.

Pines, T. (1990, January). [**Personal interview**]. Washington, DC.

Pool, I. (1979). Direct broadcast satellites and the integrity of national cultures. In K. Nordenstreng and H. Schiller (Eds.), **National sovereignty and international communication.** Norwood, NJ: Ablex Publishing Company.

Pool, J. (1964). **The propaganda factor in Russian history.** (Dissertation). Washington, DC: Georgetown University.

Propaganda analysis. (1938). New York: Institute for Propaganda Analysis, Inc.

Rabida, A. (1943). **The use of propaganda as a weapon in warfare.** (Dissertation). Washington, DC: Georgetown University.

Randolph, E. (1988, June 1). USIA's Worldnet promotes good guys, but who's watching. **The Washington Post,** A17.

Ray, E. & Preston, W. (1983). Disinformation and mass deception: Democracy as a cover story. **Covert Action Information Bulletin,** 19, 3-12.

Raykov, Z. (1984). Aggression via satellite. **World Press Review,** 31, 52.

Reagan, R. (1987). **Public diplomacy in the information age.** Washington, DC: United States Advisory Commission on Public Diplomacy Conference.

Regan, D. (1984). [**Letter to Charles Z. Wick**]. Washington,

D.C: The Secretary of the Treasury.

Response to staff investigation of USIA's Worldnet operations in London, Paris, and Brussels: Subcommittee on International Operations, Committee on Foreign Affairs, House of Representatives. (1986). Washington, DC: United States. Information Agency.

Richardson, C. (1977). In United States House of Representatives. Subcommittee on International Operations, Committee on International Operations. Hearings. Public diplomacy and the future. (June 8-24). Washington, DC: United States Government Printing Office.

Righetti, S. (1993, February). [Personal interview]. Former Technical Information Specialist, United States Information Agency. Washington, DC.

Roett, R. (1977). In United States House of Representatives. Subcommittee on International Operations, Committee on International Operations. Hearings. Public diplomacy and the future. (June 8-24). Washington, DC: United States Government Printing Office.

Rogerson, S. (1938). Propaganda in the next war. London: MacKays Limited.

Roth, L. (1980). Public diplomacy and the past: The studies of U.S. information and cultural programs (1952-1975). Executive Seminar in National and International Affairs. Washington, DC: United States Department of State, Foreign Service Institute.

Roth, L. (1984). Public diplomacy and the past: The search for an American style of propaganda (1952-1977). **The Fletcher Forum, 8,** 353-391.

Rowson, R. (1966). The American commitment to private international political communications: A view of Free Europe, Inc. **Law and Contemporary Problems, 31,** 458-472.

Rubin, B. (1960). **Realities, images, and psychological warfare: 1945-1956.** Boston, MA; Boston University.

Ruth, D. (1987, November 22). Worldnet specializes in softselling of America. **Chicago Sun Times, 35,** 38.

Ryan, L. (1977). In United States House of Representatives. Subcommittee on International Operations, Committee on International Operations. Hearings. **Public diplomacy and the future.** (June 8-24). Washington, DC: United States Government Printing Office.

Sampson, S. (1980). **The crisis in American diplomacy.** North Quincy, MA: The Christopher Publishing House.

Schapiro, M. (1985). Is anybody out there watching? Charlie Wick's latest flop. **Washington Monthly, 17,** 51-52.

Short, K. (Ed.). (1983). **Film and radio propaganda in World War II.** Knoxville: University of Tennessee Press.

Shulman, H. (1990). **The Voice of America.** Madison, WI: The University of Wisconsin Press.

Simon, P. (1989). [**Letter to The Honorable Lawrence Smith**]. Washington, DC: United States Senate.

Sinai, R. (1987, July 12). **The Reagan administration's breakfast**

TV show for the world. Associated Press News Release.

Smith, B. & Smith, C. (1956). **International communication and public opinion.** Princeton, NJ: University of Princeton.

Snyder, A. (1990, January). [**Personal interview**]. Washington, DC.

Soley, L. (1989). **Radio warfare.** New York: Praeger.

Sorensen, T. (1968). **The word war: The story of American propaganda.** New York: Harper & Row.

Spreading USIA's word. (1985, February 18). **Broadcasting.**

Staar, R. (1986). **Public diplomacy: USA versus USSR.** Stanford: Hoover Institution.

Staats, E. (1977). In United States House of Representatives. Subcommittee on International Operations, Committee on International Operations. Hearings. **Public diplomacy and the future.** (June 8-24). Washington, DC: United States Government Printing Office.

Staats, E. (1979, July 23). **The public diplomacy in other countries: Implications for the United States.** Report to Congress.

Stanton, F. (1977). In United States House of Representatives. Subcommittee on International Operations, Committee on International Operations. Hearings. **Public diplomacy and the future.** (June 8-24). Washington, DC: United States Government Printing Office.

Statutory authority for the United States Advisory

Commission on Public Diplomacy. (1983). United States Advisory Commission on Public Diplomacy. Washington, DC: United States Advisory Commission on Diplomacy.

Stephens, O. (1955). **Facts to a candid world: America's overseas information program.** Stanford: Stanford University Press.

Summary of key initiatives under USIA Director Charles Z. Wick. (1988, Summer). Washington, DC: United States Information Agency.

Summers, R. (Ed.). (1951). **America's weapons of psychological warfare.** New York: The H.W. Wilson Co.

Swaebe. G. (1986, April). [**Unclassified Telegram from Brussels to the United States Information Agency**]. Washington, DC.

Sweet, W. (1981). America's information effort abroad. **Editorial Research Reports, 11,** 675-692.

Taylor, P. (1983). Propaganda in international politics. In K. Short, (Ed.), **Film and radio propaganda in World War II.** Knoxville: University of Tennessee Press.

Technology: The televised future of USIA. (1984, March 26). **Broadcasting, 651.**

Television and Film Service. (1984). **Media reaction to Worldnet.** Fact Sheet. Washington, DC: United States Information Agency.

Television and Film Service. (1985). **Worldnet.** Washington, DC: United States Information Agency.

Television and Film Service. (1989). **The Worldnet system at** the United States Information Agency's television and film service. Fact Sheet. Washington, DC: United States Information Agency.

The privatization of Europe. (1986, March 31). **Broadcasting,** 61-66.

The United States communicates with the world: A study of U.S. international information and cultural programs and activities. (1975). Washington, DC: Foreign Affairs Division, Congressional Research Service, United States Library of Congress.

Thompson, W. (1988). Anti-Americanism and the U.S. Government. **Annals of the American Academy of Political Social Science, 497,** 20-34.

To Congress about Worldnet: It's working, so let it be. (1988, June 13). Editorial. **The Providence Journal,** 2.

Toward a modern diplomacy. (1968). Washington, DC: American Foreign Service Association.

Townley, R. (1984). This is one show that's driving the Russians crazy. **TV Guide, 32,** 40-42.

United States Advisory Commission on Public Diplomacy. (1980). **Report of the United States Advisory Commission on Public Diplomacy.** Washington, DC: Government Printing Office.

United States Advisory Commission on Public Diplomacy. (1982).

Report of the United States Advisory Commission on Public Diplomacy. Washington, DC: Government Printing Office.

United States Advisory Commission on Public Diplomacy. (1983). **Report of the United States Advisory Commission on Public Diplomacy.** Washington, DC: Government Printing Office.

United States Advisory Commission on Public Diplomacy. (1985). **Report of the United States Advisory Commission on Public Diplomacy.** Washington, DC; Government Printing Office.

United States Advisory Commission on Public Diplomacy. (1986). **Report of the United States Advisory Commission on Public Diplomacy.** Washington, DC: Government Printing Office.

United States Advisory Commission on Public Diplomacy. (1989). **Report of the United States Advisory Commission on Public Diplomacy.** Washington, DC: Government Printing Office.

United States Advisory Commission on Public Diplomacy. (1990). **Public diplomacy in a new Europe.** Report of the United States Advisory Commission on Public Diplomacy. Washington, DC: Government Printing Office.

United States House of Representatives. Subcommittee on

International Operations: Committee on International Operations. (1977). Hearings. **Public diplomacy and the future.** 95th Congress. (June 8-24).

United States House of Representatives. Subcommittee on International Operations, Committee on International Operations. (1986). Hearings. **Oversight of public diplomacy.** 99th Congress. (July 16, 23; August 6; & September 6).

USIA: A battered but powerful propaganda tool. (1984, March 5). **U.S. News & World Report,** 58-61.

USIA: All the world's an audience. (1985, April 22). **Broadcasting,** 112-115.

USIA initiatives since June 9, 1981. (1988). USIA Historical Collection. Washington, DC: United States Information Agency.

USIA launches TV network. (1984, January 23). **The Asheville Times,** 20.

USIA launches TV reports in Europe. (1985, April). **The Los Angeles Times,** 3, part III.

USIA name change is only skin deep. (1983). **News Media and the Law,** 7, 33-38.

USIA solicits material to presentU.S.to the world. (1983, July 25). **Broadcasting,** 26-27.

USIA Worldnet revises game plan at first anniversary. (1986). **Television-Radio Age,** 33, 17-19.

Uttaro, R. (1982). The Voice of America in international radio propaganda. **Law and Contemporary Problems,** 45, 103-112.

Viereck, G. (1930). **Spreading germs of hate.** New York: Horace Liveright.

Voice of America, 1942-1992, 50 years of broadcasting to the world. (1992). Washington, DC: United States Information Agency.

Walker, F. (1982). PYSOP is a nasty term-too bad. In R. Laurin (Ed.), **Military propaganda, psychological warfare, and operations.** New York: Praeger.

Ward, P. (1977). In United States House of Representatives. Subcommittee on International Operations, Committee on International Operations. Hearings. **Public diplomacy and the future.** (June 8-24). Washington, DC; United States Government Printing Office.

Ward, J., Pool, I., & Solomon, R. (1983). **A study of future directions for the Voice of America in the changing world of international broadcasting.** Cambridge, MA: MIT.

Warlaumont, H. (1988). Strategies in international radio wars: A comparative approach. **Journal of Broadcasting & Electronic Media, 32,** 43-59.

Websters Ninth New Collegiate Dictionary. (1989). Springfield, MA: Merriam-Webster Inc.

Weinraub, B. (1986, December 29). Information chief who stays close to Reagan; working profile. **New York Times, 138,** B10.

White, R. (1958). Resistance to international propaganda. In W.E. Daugherty (Ed.), **A psychological warfare casebook.** Baltimore: John Hopkins University Press.

Whitton, J. (1963). **Propaganda and the cold war.** Washington, DC: Public Affairs Press.

Whitton, J. (1966). The problem of curbing international propaganda. **Law and Contemporary Problems, 31,** 601-621.

Wick, C. (1987). [**Letter to President Reagan**]. USIA Historical Collection. Washington, DC: United States Information Agency.

Wick, C. (1988). [**Letter to The Honorable Claiborne Pell, Chairman, Committee on Foreign Relations, United States Senate**]. USIA Historical Collection. Washington, DC: United States Information Agency.

Wick, C. (1990, January). [**Personal interview**]. Los Angeles, CA.

Wick, C. (1992, March). [**Personal interview**]. Los Angeles, CA.

Wick legacy: Making a difference. (1988, November 7). **Broadcasting, 115,** 43-44.

Wick proposes Soviet-U.S. TV exchange. (1985, February 18). **Broadcasting, 72.**

Wick urges approval of USIA budget in light of Soviet activity. (1986, March 31). **Broadcasting, 110,** 82-83.

Wick, Worldnet and the war of ideas. (1986, November 3). **Broadcasting, 78.**

Woodring, P. (1977). In United States House of Representatives. Subcommittee on International Operations, Committee on International Operations. Hearings. **Public diplomacy and** the future. (June 8-24). Washington, DC: United States Government Printing Office.

World TV network begun to explain American policy. (1984, January 23). **Pennsylvania News, 936,** 35.

Worldnet-2/Euronet-2. **Reactions.** (1983). USIA Historical Collection. Washington, DC: United States Information Agency.

Worldnet-4/Euronet-4. **Reactions.** (1983). USIA Historical Collection. Washington, DC: United States Information Agency.

Worldnet-9/Euronet-9. **Reactions.** (1983). USIA Historical Collection. Washington, DC: United States Information Agency.

Worldnet-10/Euronet-10. **Reactions.** (1983). USIA Historical Collection. Washington, DC: United States Information Agency.

Worldnet-11/Euronet-11. Reactions. (1983). USIA Historical Collection. Washington, DC: United States Information Agency.

Worldnet-15/Euronet-15. **Reactions.** (1984). USIA Historical Collection. Washington, DC: United States Information Agency.

Worldnet-16/Arnet-1. **Reactions.** (1984). USIA Historical Collection. Washington, DC: United States Information Agency.

Worldnet-17/Euronet-16. **Reactions.** (1984). USIA Historical

Collection. Washington, DC: United States Information Agency.

Worldnet, a report. (1985). Report prepared by Charles Wick and USIA Staff for the House Foreign Affairs Committee. Washington, DC: USIA.

Worldnet: A way for the U.S. to tell its story abroad – quickly. (1984). **U.S. News and World Report, 96,** 61.

Worldnet broadcasts to USSR near. (1988). **Television Digest,** 5-7.

Worldnet budget hit. (1987, December 21). **Television Digest, 5+.**

Worldnet expanding global satellite program service. (1986, April 26). **Broadcast Daily, 5+.**

Worldnet fact sheet. (1984). USIA Historical Collection. Washington, DC: United States Information Agency.

Worldnet: February 1987 update. (1987). Washington, DC: United States Information Agency.

Worldnet goes to Latin America, Eastern Europe. (1991, February 11). **Broadcasting, 120,** 76.

Worldnet opens doors to the South. (1986, October 21). **Broadcasting,** 52-54.

Worldnet: Putting satellite technology to work for global understanding. (1988). Washington, DC: United States Information Agency.

Worldnet: Secondary usage. (1988). Washington, DC: United States Information Agency.

Worldnet: The first five years. (1989, January). [From the personal library of Charles Z. Wick]. Los Angeles, CA.

Worldnet viewership around the world. (1989). Washington, DC: United States Information Agency.

Zettl, H. (1984). Television production handbook. Belmount, California: Wadsworth Publishing Company.

Zimmerman, R. (1985, February 13). Soviets asked to share in TV newscasts. Ohio Dealer, 27.

About the Author

An internationally accredited business communicator and certified development project manager, Donna is the author of numerous articles and three books including *The Value of Water: A Compendium of Essays by Smart CEOs*. Donna has worked previously as a management and branding consultant for international organizations and is globally recognized as a champion for water, sustainability, agriculture and the environment. She was one of 10 social scientists to conduct research in world capitals for the U.S. Treasury's first redesign of the $100 bill.

As Chief of Party for the Securing Water for Food Technical Assistance Facility, a multi-lateral government-funded, incubator-accelerator, she is a catalyzing social impact entrepreneurship in the water-ag nexus. She holds a Ph.D. in international communication, has worked and travelled in nearly 40 countries, and appreciates being called a multipotentialite.

Notes

www.ingramcontent.com/pod-product-compliance
Lightning Source LLC
Chambersburg PA
CBHW070920270326
41927CB00011B/2655